ALCOHOLISM IN AMERICA

ALCOHOLISM IN AMERICA

HARRISON M. TRICE
Cornell University

ROBERT E. KRIEGER PUBLISHING COMPANY
HUNTINGTON, NEW YORK
1978

Original Edition 1966
Reprint 1978 with new preface

Printed and Published by
ROBERT E. KRIEGER PUBLISHING CO., INC.
645 NEW YORK AVENUE
HUNTINGTON, NEW YORK 11743

Copyright © 1966 by
McGRAW—HILL BOOK COMPANY
Reprinted by Arrangement

Library of Congress Cataloging in Publication Data

Trice, Harrison Miller, 1920-
  Alcoholism in America.

  Reprint of the ed. published by McGraw-Hill, New York,
in series: McGraw-Hill social problems series.
  Includes bibliographical references and index.
  1. Liquor problem--United States. 2. Alcoholism--
United States. I. Title.
(HV5292.T7   1978)   362.2'92'0973   77-2665
ISBN 0-88275-479-3

Over 40,000 articles on alcoholism abstracted from the world's literature are on file at the Alcoholism Research Center at Rutgers University. This large number indicates the broad interest of modern societies in alcohol consumption and their concern for its implications for human behavior.

Professor Trice confines his presentation to the American society, and the portrait he presents of alcohol, alcoholism, and the alcoholic person probably differs only very slightly from that found in other industrialized societies. One simple finding, dramatic in spite of its obviousness, is the widespread acceptance of the use of alcohol. Bread and wine have truly become the staff of life in modern societies, and stigmatization of the alcohol user, at least of the moderate user, has largely disappeared. In contrast, opiates and their users, called addicts, are viewed completely negatively. Opiates are not readily available; their use is largely forbidden and is considered morally reprehensible. The addict who is "hooked" is considered a dangerous deviant who must be restrained, punished, and often incarcerated away from society in a total institution.

Alcohol, in the many forms produced for consumption, is legally sanctified and is a multibillion dollar economic enterprise. If for any reason the sale of alcoholic beverages were forbidden, large segments of the working population would be in dire economic straits. Persons engaged primarily in the production, distribution, and sale of beverages would be without jobs. Dislocation of the national economy and the collapse of major economic institutions would be inevitable. The distillery industry today is a basic enterprise integrated into the fabric of the total economy. There is little prospect that our government, the public, business, or industry would tolerate any curtailment of alcoholic beverage production any more than they would limit the production of tobacco goods or automobiles.

The alcohol consumer is placed in a peculiar position: The alcohol industry has big business status, but at the same time the product is habit-forming and can lead the individual consumer into a deviant position in society. The individual is left to rely upon his own resources, specifically his ability to restrain himself and to drink in moderation and under appropriate conditions. The alcohol industry and social control agencies, such as the police, preach the theme of moderation and engage in special pleadings and warnings to citizens especially around the holiday season: "If you drink, do not drive"; "Alcohol and driving do not mix"; "Do not be the slob at the party," etc.

Leaving it up to the individual to handle his drinking of alcoholic beverages is understandable even though probably unworkable for a number of imbibers. Self-control and self-mastery are long-held ideals in American culture. To be unable to control situations and one's activity within them is a sign of moral weakness. The individual of strong moral fiber who can control his own destiny is believed to be a desired prototype for all individuals in the society. It is not unusual, therefore, for persons in the late stages of alcoholism to deny the need for help or even to reject it when offered by family members, friends, or social and rehabilitation agencies. The individual who cannot control his drinking experiences in time so strong a social segregation from society that his only alternative is to accept this deviant status and to seek comfort among others in a similar condition. The society has labeled him an alcoholic, thus stigmatizing and segregating him, and he reacts by a form of self-segregation. He joins the company of other drinkers who as a group isolate themselves from "normal" society.

Professor Trice traces admirably the movement of the individual through the various stages of alcoholism and the individual and institutional responses to the behaviors accompanying this movement. He begins his analysis with the initial observation that some individuals can handle the need to drink and the amount consumed while others cannot. The best explanation is personality. Drinking affects emotional behavior. It can serve as a depressant for some individuals and a stimulant for others, depending upon the personality makeup of the individual. It can be a tranquilizer for some persons and can in others produce a heightened excitement whereby learned inhibitions are reduced and emotional expressions are effusive and free. The ego is exposed, unprotected. Apparently the use of alcohol and the amounts consumed are related to the biological, genetic, and personality endowment of the individual. What is difficult to determine is a clear-cut relationship between the amount of intake of alcohol and behavior. Is this effect upon behavior due to conditioning, experience, genetic endowment, biological makeup, and such variables as age or sex? Stated simply, why does the drinking of one ounce of alcohol release the libido in one individual while it may have no effect upon another? Why are six ounces necessary to produce the effect in a third person? The answer is not forthcoming easily because of the involvement of so many complex biological, genetic, psychological, and social factors.

Professor Trice also analyzes the increased opportunity today to have drinking experiences and to receive group support for such activities. The messages of the alcohol beverage industries are virtually unrestricted in the mass media, and the public is saturated with paid and unpaid commercials regarding the availability and the proper and sophisticated use of spirits. At one time drinking groups were largely identified with ethnic and cultural minorities, but today there are all sorts of groups, from bunny clubs to commuter-train-bar clubs. The price of admission is the price of a drink and reasonable behavior. When the drinker cannot afford the price or when his behavior becomes unreasonable, he can find another group and a lower-priced firewater.

A fascinating and almost insoluble problem for the drinker and nondrinker alike is the vacillation and ambivalence with which drinking is viewed in our society and the extreme stigmatization, isolation, and oftentimes punishment of the late-stage drinker who has lost self-control. The illogic of this situation, as Professor Trice indicates, is that before the individual becomes labeled an alcoholic nothing is done for him, and no appropriate behavioral guidelines exist for the individual who is moving into increasing dependency upon alcohol for a sense of well-being. Prior to the deterioration of his role performance as a husband, father, and worker, neither he nor the "significant others" in his life realize (perhaps care) or recognize his illness for what it is and will become. However, once he has crossed the Rubicon into the land of the obsessed drinker, he is "treated" and often rejected by family members and colleagues in his work.

Trice emphasizes the persistence of the norm of self-control and the effects of a pervading adherence to this norm upon the drinker and the nondrinker. This norm is one crucial criterion in the drinking person's evaluation of himself and leads inevitably to a shattered self-image and indulgence in self-pity as the incipient alcoholic experiences loss of control with his increasing dependence on alcohol.

It would be extremely helpful if alcoholism were treated as an illness and the alcoholic as a patient. Persons who are the "significant others" in the drinker's life could act according to a set of well-articulated and understood norms to cure the ailment and to return the individual to his normal role in society. Unfortunately, if drinking per se is an illness, it is regarded as a benign or "good" illness and becomes acute, requiring immediate attention, only when the drinker becomes a problem to himself, to his family, and to the caretakers of society. In other words a social definition of alcoholism as an illness prevails, and when the individual has such troubles as absenteeism from work, wife beating, and delirium tremens, the diagnosis is made and treatment follows. In most instances diagnosis and treatment at this stage are too late to help the individual. Restoration therapy is a time-consuming and costly process.

It is quite clear in Professor Trice's presentation that alcohol has a functional place in a variety of business and leisure situations. The functional significance of drinking in American life is likely to increase rather than to lessen; hence, the need to educate our society to the false promises of emotional and social gratification offered by alcoholism. The traits of those who might find more than usual gratification in drinking and thus be especially vulnerable to addiction deserve thorough study. The symptoms of a person progressing into middle and late stages of alcoholism; and the alternative means of preventing, arresting, and treating alcoholism also need continuing investigation. The crux of the matter, as Trice states it, is to provide controls for an incipient alcoholic within society rather than to allow him to reach a point of deviance at which he is totally excluded from society and from his supportive primary relationships.

The paradoxes and complexities of the alcoholism problem almost defy explanation, but Professor Trice probes, digests, and integrates disparate facts with the resultant inescapable conclusion that no one class, racial, ethnic, or economic group has a monopoly on alcoholics and their problems. Drinking is a universal practice in American society, and it means different things to different groups and individuals.

Despite these differences, such as Orthodox Jews engaging largely in ceremonial drinking, Italians drinking as part of a meal, and the French drinking as a social necessity—all drinkers value independence in the indulgence or control of the impulse. This is a reflection of middle-class values and is one of the paradoxes. Alcohol functions as a facilitator of social exchange; it allows people to relate to others in a primary group— a need sorely felt in "a complex society where impersonal competitive living prevails." But it is left up to the individual to control his drinking, an almost impossible achievement for the heavy drinker, and thus he is presented with a dilemma. He has no "clear negative sanctions" regarding social drinking, but when he becomes a "problem drinker" he fights the individuals and social agencies which attempt to help him. In obtaining a mandate to imbibe freely, he almost feels obligated to abide by the norm of independence and self-control. This is the paradox.

Alcohol can function as a tranquilizer or as a means of "changing reality." Minority groups, according to Professor Trice, especially lower-class Negroes and other new migrants from rural areas recently arrived in the city, are drawn to heavy drinking for this reason. As these groups become mobile and take on middle-class values, they identify with the Protestant ethic that to drink is to give in to weakness and impulse, and they do so with guilt feelings over the loss of self-control.

The heavy drinkers of the middle class, more than those of any other social class, suffer the greatest psychological stress and least societal control over their behavior. They are plagued with guilt feelings about their drinking because they have given in to impulse. They struggle constantly for restoration to the former state of self-control, and they become deluded into believing they have obtained rehabilitation through self-mastery of their problem and consequently avoid all forms of help from family, friends, and social agencies. When they are "middle-stage alcoholics," according to Professor Trice, "because of their comparative stability, and because of 'significant others' who absorb their behavior and vacillate about taking firm action, they are relatively invisible and do not run high risks of being arrested or committed to state hospitals."

The number of problem drinkers, 4,500,000 in 1960, with the greatest percentage found among workers in the productive years (thirty-five to fifty), should interest the student in such questions as the following: Is there the need for a national policy and program to curtail excessive drinking in order to reduce its deleterious effects on role functioning in the family, work, and community? Is the incidence of alcoholism (number of new alcoholics during a given period of time, usually expressed in rates per thousand individuals who are in the universe of actual or potential drinkers) increasing each year and among what age group? Is sex an important factor? Do more men than women become alcoholics? Is the incidence rate changing for women? The student should note that Professor Trice dramatizes the consequences for the family when a breadwinner becomes an alcoholic. The space limitations of this volume have prevented a full treatment of the woman alcoholic in the family, of how this condition impairs her marriage possibilities (if single), and how it may lead to various types of deviant behavior such as prostitution or drug addiction. The married woman alcoholic can be severely impaired in her role performance, especially in the socialization tasks, and can often delimit her husband's occupational and social mobility.

Rehabilitation of the individual suffering from any disabling illness takes a long period of time, is extremely costly, and often taxes the patience of the most highly motivated and dedicated members of organizations engaged in therapy. The problem of rehabilitating the alcoholic is even more complicated. First, it is hard to find him and to get him to seek aid. He has the opportunity to belong to a variety of drinking groups. If the members of one group find his drinking a problem and suggest to him that "he do something about it," he is most likely to seek and find rather easily a more deviant group which accepts his obsessed behavior. This rapid mobility from one imbiber group to another prevents his "controlled" and good-mannered drinking colleagues from routing him to sources of aid in the early stage of his alcoholic career, a stage during which he can most likely be rehabilitated and with minimum cost.

A related difficulty which complicates rehabilitation of the alcoholic is the uncertainty regarding the effectiveness of treatment strategies currently in use. Is the strategy of complete abstinence from drinking best for all individuals? Is "constructive coercion" more likely to work with individuals who respond to authority and the admonitions of those they admire than with those who are more individualistic in their behavior and rebellious by temperament? Group therapy appears to be most effective in the treatment of alcoholism. The place of the individual-treatment strategy in the therapy process, however, remains to be determined. An individualized program of rehabilitation is tailored to the individual's personality configuration, his social values, and previous experiences as a problem drinker. For achieving certain objectives—such as improving one's views of oneself, learning how to live with a problem, discovering that other individuals are fellow sufferers, group programs such as those provided by AA are very successful. For other objectives, such as changing the course of the illness, in this instance alcoholism, a more handcrafted therapy program is required. In a group session in which the consequences of excessive drinking are being discussed an individual may perceive the discussion as a threat, a form of coercion, a tongue-lashing, or as a bit of good advice. He may respond by compliance with the prescribed therapy or by overindulgence in alcohol.

The same set of reactions may occur in a one-to-one relationship between a physician and his patient. A heavy drinker, told by his physician that continuation of current rate of drinking will cause cirrhosis of the liver within six months, may fearfully stop drinking completely or may assume the attitude, "I will stop drinking tomorrow," and overcome his sorrows and anxieties by going on a drinking binge. This last example points to the need to assess the individual's psychological and biological makeup and his readiness to accept the appropriate therapy.

The basic need in alcoholism rehabilitation is to provide the drinker with at least one new role with which he identifies, which has meaning to him, and in which he believes he excels over all others. One hope for effecting resocialization of the alcoholic into one or more new roles is the current posture of industry and labor in our society. Professor Trice suggests that "company-based personnel policies and programs on alcoholism offer the main opportunity for making realistic progress against alcoholism." ". . . The alcoholic's boss is a neutral 'significant other' who could effectively recognize and control the illness in its early stage." The "long arm of the job" is a powerful influence in our society, and if early rehabilitation cannot begin in the drinker's work situation, then it is most likely not to begin at all. The task is to provide alternatives to excessive drinking which are rewarding and which provide the motivation to substitute a more positive role for a deviant one.

Professor Trice discusses such problems. He answers some questions but raises many others. This is his task. In a short work on an involved and complicated subject one can only tease the reader to seek the facts, raise the relevant questions, postulate the theories, and perhaps do some research. That is why we have universities, colleges, and libraries.

Marvin B. Sussman

ACKNOWLEDGMENTS

Within the usual confusions of academic life—teaching, ongoing research, and adult offerings—it is not too difficult to bring together materials and get them into a rough manuscript form. It is an entirely different matter, however, to find the time, to say nothing of the patience, necessary to refine and edit. I have, therefore, been most fortunate in having the help of Mrs. Norma Landen, Administrative Aide, "Alcoholism and Occupational Health" Project, whose keen eye and word-economy have been of inestimable value to me in this manuscript. Appreciation is also extended to Paul Roman, who critically commented on the manuscript and prepared the index. In addition, Mrs. Marilyn Hickok has been an unerring and all-patient typist.

Harrison M. Trice

Many developments have occurred on the "drug scene" since this little book was first published in 1966. For example, a new generation, and now its "new generation", has explored, used, and abused a wide variety of drugs other than alcohol. The federal government, through the National Institute of Alcoholism and Alcohol Abuse, has poured literally millions into a national effort to explain, prevent, and treat alcohol dependency. Currently there is an unprecedented "boom" in efforts to set in motion job-based programs for problem-drinking employees. Literally thousands of persons now claim to be "counselors" and "therapists", and the number of treatment facilities have also increased by the thousands. All clamor to be called "professionals" and to be "accredited". All seem to try very hard to devise "new ways" and compete strenuously to outdo one another.

Despite these and many other efforts and trends, there remains, today, as in 1966, a large, persistent, and wide-spread population of alcohol abusers which now includes the multiple drug abuser, among whom women predominate, and those "potheads" who have come to abuse marihuana, often in conjunction with alcohol. Never mind the debates over how many. They are legion—in the millions—and there are no reasons to believe their legions have decreased. On the contrary, there is every reason to believe they have increased, the most prominent reason being the millions of women who now drink alcohol like men, abuse alcohol in ever increasing numbers, and who show signs of soon reaching a questionable "equity" with men in this severe public health problem. Furthermore those new generations since 1966 have continued to use alcohol in many of the ways their parents did, with the exception that they have not replaced alcohol but have tended to *join* its use with marihuana and other drugs. In short, alcohol continues to be our national drug and its abuse continues to be a severe national health problem despite a decade that saw intensified efforts and major campaigns to "do something" about alcoholism.

There is, in short, genuine cause for pessimism. Certainly the notion of "prevention" has typically been dealt with in a manner that can best be described as "well-intended"; from an uncharitable viewpoint these efforts can be seen as naive even nonsensical. Treatment remains fractured into many partisans who rarely have systematic, well designed, evaluation plans for accumulating a body of knowledge about what specific intervention works with whom, under what conditions, and for how long. Concepts about how to explain the phenomenon of deviant drinking, also remain quite undeveloped—almost in the state they were in a decade ago despite the flood of literature that eulogizes the medical model, on the one hand, and on the other, insists that alcoholism is a multi-dimensional set of behaviors, calling for interdiscipline approaches.

It is at this point that reissuance of this book seems appropriate. Without disparaging in any way the disease concept of alcoholism, this book seeks to underscore that there are sociological properties of the drug alcohol just as there are physiological and psychological ones. That is, even though there may well be physiological changes that mark the onset of full-blown alcoholism, these were probably often preceeded and accompanied by the social forces described herein. At least, the multidimensional approach which seems to be quite current today suggests this would be the case. In sum, this approach simply says that there are biological and psychological predispositions and vulnerabilities to alcoholism. These are typically made manifest and active, however, by social forces such as the drinking group processes and segregating pressures. This book explores these latter social forces and, at the same time, describes the nature of the predisposers.

Thus the conceptualization of the relationship between drinking and drinking problems is the book's major focus and the reason for its second printing. It seems reasonable to believe that in the long run progress will be made by formulating and testing concepts that stimulate new approaches and the revival and examination of past ones. Certainly all will agree that we badly need concepts that explain the set of behaviors called alcoholism in as much detail as possible before long range progress can occur. To ignore the societal forces described in this book would be to blind ourselves to a reality that, for most observers, makes a significant contribution to the final product—an abuse of alcohol that destroys the ability of an individual to meet their most basic social expectations in home, job, and community. The passage of twelve years has in no way altered the cogency of these forces. It has, however, made for a simple restatement of them. Hence the reprinting of this paperback.

A less profound, but nevertheless important reason for reissue is that the essence of some of the main issues surrounding alcoholism in American society are sketched out here: therapies and basic ways for evaluating them; job-based programs and their strategies, including "crisis precipitation"; and the essential definitions of alcoholism.

All things considered the concepts and themes are quite relevant today, as ten years ago, for the interested student who wishes to gain an overview and, at the same time, grasp a review of the main societal dynamics moving vulnerable persons into alcohol abuse.

Harrison M. Trice

CONTENTS

CONTENTS

AN OVERVIEW
OF MAIN THEMES

To explore alcoholism in America, this book uses certain basic themes. In being applied to specific use, however, these themes are often overshadowed by the facts that accompany them. For example, the symptoms that mark the progression of the disorder—such as the hangover misery of alcoholism's middle stage—are so intriguing that one tends to overlook the process of social segregation of the developing alcoholic that is also taking place. The same is true when alcoholism is compared with opiate addiction. We are likely to become engrossed in the details of dependency on opiates and to overlook the basic differences and similarities. Consequently it is important to pull out the unifying concepts in advance and state them explicitly so that they are not lost in detail. Probably more important, however, is the need to emphasize *explanatory notions* of empirical reality rather than reality itself. For these reasons the main themes underlying this study of alcoholism in America will be set forth as an introduction.

NOTE: Footnoted references, numbered consecutively by chapter, appear at the end of the book.

SOCIOCULTURAL PATTERNS AND ALCOHOLISM: THE PREDOMINANT THEMES

Alcoholism in American society is a mixture of the following chief factors: (1) prone personalities who imbibe regularly in (2) drinking groups that reflect the functional value of alcohol in a complex society, but which exercise (3) widely varying norms about what is deviant drinking behavior—a social ambivalence. As a result there are (4) weak social controls, since a deviant drinker in one group can readily move to a set of drinking companions with more tolerant norms. Finally, cultural values stressing the importance of self-control justify (5) a pattern of segregation of those who regularly become intoxicated. Chapters 2, 3, and 4 explore these factors in detail.

Vulnerable Personalities and Drinking Groups

Cultural values play a prominent role in producing alcoholism-prone personalities. American culture places stress on the sanctity of the individual and on his independence as a free responsible agent. He is, however, ideally expected to be restrained, not by external forces and pressure outside himself, but by his own self-control. Thus Americans desire to think of themselves as self-reliant, in control of their emotions, and exercising will power, qualities demanded for occupational success and competitive achievements of all kinds.

On the other hand, American parents, especially middle-class ones, believe in an absorbing kind of parental love that, if exaggerated, encourages in their children a strong dependency on the parents. This value clashes directly with individualism. As a child matures, a direct and unresolvable conflict may come from thinking of himself as independent and self-reliant, on the one hand, but highly dependent on mother, on the other. For a personality with a high degree of anxiety about his self-esteem resulting from such an independence-dependence conflict, alcohol can be very satisfying.

Before proceeding, we should sound a sharp caution about the exposure of persons to certain cultural values. In no way can any cultural value be considered universal within American society. Individual Americans differ widely in how much they learn and act upon any given value and on the extent of value conflict they experience. On the other hand, cultural values are diffused enough so that many people come under their influence. It is where conflicting cultural patterns differentially accumulate within the socialization of a given person that they contribute to alcoholism proneness.

Personality predispositions, however, are insufficient to explain alcoholism in America. They must be linked with influences that press the latent predispositions toward actual addiction. Certain qualities of many drinking groups in American society seem to do this: They legitimate the use of an anxiety-reducing drug, provide the temporary intimacy of pseudoprimary groups, give a sense of status and ego satisfaction, and allow for relaxed interaction free of threats to self-esteem. For the vulnerable personality these features are attractive and emotionally rewarding. Repeated participation in such groups accentuates the use of alcohol as the way to manage psychic tensions, exclusive of other possibilities.

Ambivalence and Weak Social Controls

Drinking groups, however, vary widely in the rules they generate to define acceptable drinking behavior. In the past, as well as at the present time, American society has been deeply ambivalent about what alcohol's effects should mean. Lying behind this lack of uniformity are cultural confusions about drinking norms. The American temperance movement produced conflicts which still continue to fracture attitudes about alcohol into many camps. The entire prohibition movement turned drinking into an intense moral issue and made complete abstinence a norm of behavior for thousands of Protestant Americans.

Ethnic pluralism fostered other norms about alcohol's meaning.[1] For example, among Jewish-Americans alcohol drinking is a symbolic act in a series of religious rituals. From such a drinking pattern emerged a ritual norm which, rather than saying "Thou shalt not," as in the abstinence norm, says in effect, "Drink in a certain way for a certain meaning."

Still other subcultures manifest different definitions of alcohol's effects. A convivial norm—the belief that the emotional effects of alcohol promote group cohesiveness—exists among many native American, Scandinavian, and German segments. This norm, which often applies to cocktail parties, suggests that alcohol's effects allow persons who scarcely know one another to be friendly, outgoing, and part of a group.

A utilitarian meaning permeates still other large parts of our complex American society. It fosters the notion that alcohol provides the drinker with some personal advantage primarily for himself. It urges him to use alcohol to reduce his anxieties, stresses, and conflicts. Consequently heavy drinking is often encouraged as a guideline for drinking behavior. Irish attitudes toward alcohol often have such a meaning.

We might also speak of a dietary norm, when alcohol is seen merely as a supplement to meals. Among first-generation Italians wine was regarded as a food along with other foodstuffs and nothing more.

In sum, alcohol and its effects never remain undefined. Inevitably social values of a particular group give the drinker some kind of meaning for what alcohol does for him. Since in the United States no one of these norms consistently prevails, uniform social controls over the use of alcohol are weakened. Many Americans may follow more than one set of rules concerning drinking. A person may adhere to one set of rules in his family, another with his work associates, and still another when he is "out on the town." In each group he faces different rewards and punishments.

Many groups have no rules regarding drinking per se, but most come to reject a drinker as a future drinking companion due to certain kinds of drinking conduct: vulgarity, open aggression, sexual advances, excessive hilarity. At the same time the degree of acceptance before rejection varies widely between groups. Thus, if a developing alcoholic's drinking behavior violates the norms of a rather conservative group, he can find emotional rewards by affiliating with more lenient sets of drinking companions. In the process his dependence on alcohol increases, but he is not confronted by realistic social controls with clear negative sanctions.

Patterns of Segregation

Finally, as the alcoholic drinks more and more with other heavy drinkers, an irreversible reaction by the general community segregates him from "normal" drinkers. At such a degree of deviation, the broad cultural value of self-reliance and self-control justifies a segregation which frees him even further from effective social controls over his drinking. In short, recurrent loss of self-discipline because of drinking calls for social avoidance and systematic rejection. The exclusion process, however, now gives the alcoholic deviant roles within highly stigmatized groups and encourages him to fulfill them.

ALCOHOL AND EMOTIONAL BEHAVIOR

Another theme which we must discuss in exploring alcoholism is the effects of alcohol on individual emotional behavior. The subject is not covered in any one particular chapter, but its importance is recognized in every area of our study. We must note that discreet human behavior is a varying combination of physical response, intelligence, learned abilities, emotions, and social values which differ in each individual.

Because individuals also differ in their tolerance of alcohol, it is difficult to generalize about how alcohol's internal effects will emerge in external individual behavior. The fact is known that, taken rapidly in large amounts, not only does alcohol seriously impair skills, learning, and perception, but it renders the individual practically helpless. Most people, however, drink in relatively diluted and small quantities, approaching only a degree of drunkenness. How do alcohol's physical effects influence behavior in these usual situations? For some persons, small and moderate amounts improve specific task performance. Emotionally, some personalities become quarrelsome, some overtalkative, and others weepy and maudlin. Apparently, therefore, alcohol's effects on behavior are more complex than is usually believed.[2] We can only conclude that if the drinker imbibes large amounts, typical effects on behavior can be observed, but that when relatively small amounts are imbibed, no typical behavior pattern emerges.

However, some cautious, limited statements about emotional behavior do have meaning. Although alcohol's influence on emotional behavior is only partly understood today, apparently it does act to reduce the tensions of confusion, threat, and anxiety, as has been shown by Greenberg.[3] Experiments with both animals and humans have suggested breakups of anxiety symptoms by alcohol. The animal studies further suggest that having experienced a lessening of these painful emotions via alcohol, the animal turns more and more to alcoholic beverages.

In this perspective alcohol is both helpful and harmful. Taken in moderate amounts, it serves as a tranquilizer for those with normal stresses, aiding adjustment. For those with neurotic traits of intense anxiety it may temporarily reduce these, helping the emotionally handicapped person to perform for the time being. But such use, over the long run, exposes this drinker to dependence on alcohol.

Studies also suggest that alcohol acts to reduce learned inhibitions.[4] In the process of growing up, everyone learns control and masking of feelings, but moderate amounts of alcohol relax these superego restraints, loosening the grip of the conscious mind on emotions usually held in check. As control on behavior weakens, the negative censor that is sober judgment relaxes, leading to a mild euphoria. Thus the drinker metaphorically puts on rose-colored glasses, while reality tends to recede into the background.

It is clear from these points that some personalities may get more unusual emotional rewards from drinking alcohol than do others. Those with intense feelings of worthlessness and inadequacy will tend to be temporarily relieved of these anxieties by moderate to heavy amounts of alcohol. In addition, alcohol will probably further reduce their learned inhibitions so that they can experience the excitement of antisocial behavior.

IMPACT ON PIVOTAL INSTITUTIONS

Alcoholism affects numerous people other than the suffering alcoholic himself. Chapter 5 summarizes some of the main problems created by alcoholism at home and at work. Probably the main impact which the alcoholic has on his home and his job is impaired role performance. Whether husband and father or wife and mother, the alcoholic fails to fill the minimum expected of him in either role. Although he enters marriage at about the same rate as others, he fails at the role, as his high rate of broken marriages indicates. Though he works during most of his alcoholism, his work performance steadily deteriorates despite flurries of effective performance.

Furthermore, for both spouse and immediate boss, the alcoholic is a source of emotional trauma. As a spouse goes through the alcoholism progression with his or her alcoholic mate, he increasingly shows signs of neurotic and disturbed behavior. Supervisors and union stewards experience the alcoholic as a first-class supervisory problem to which they must devote much time. All three of these "significant others"—spouse, union official, and boss—find themselves in unstructured situations, in which they hesitate to confront, try to manage the problem themselves without outside help, and are generally indecisive. Because they implicitly believe the drinker must parallel the behavior of the skid-row bum before they take action, the social controls potentially present in these three key figures are delayed and weakened.

NEED FOR PERSPECTIVE: COMPARISON WITH OPIATE ADDICTION

Further to explore alcoholism in America, we must emphasize what could be called a "perspective" theme. Most discussions of alcoholism remain within a narrow focus on alcohol pathology. In order, however, fully to understand alcoholism, it should be compared with other addictions. Since comparison would probably be aided most by contrast with another drug addiction, Chapter 6 concentrates on the differences between and similarities of alcoholism and opiate dependency.

Unlike alcohol drinking, opiate use has scant social ambivalence connected with it. Opiates have no well-defined functions in American society as does alcohol. On the contrary, there is a widespread and uniform belief that to use opiates is reprehensible, except, perhaps, within the bottommost segments of American society. Even here there are reasons to believe that many look upon opiate use as repulsive. These uniform social controls contribute to the comparatively small numbers of addicts in America. These are confined largely to persons in the lowest strata.

NEED FOR EVALUATION: THE SCIENTISTS ENTER THE PICTURE

The fact that the drinking of alcohol is a moral, emotionally charged issue in American society is another theme we cannot overlook in the exploration of alcoholism. For almost a century the temperance movement waged a heated, widespread, and well-supported campaign to prohibit legally the drinking of alcohol. In the process any objective and systematic effort to study alcohol and alcoholism became practically impossible.

Within the past twenty-five years, however, scientists from many different disciplines have started to study alcoholism's numerous facets. Repeal of national prohibition in 1933 caused a mild demise in the intense, morally oriented argument over alcohol's meaning. Then the Great Depression of the 1930s took precedence over the battle of prohibition and its repeal, and later, World War II served further to hold in abeyance the moral struggle over alcohol and alcoholism. Apparently this time-out period permitted the emergence of a more objective and scientifically oriented approach. Certainly the interest in and study of alcoholism since World War II have been generally different from what they were during the heyday of the temperance forces. The chief difference lies in the rise of a sizable group of physical and social scientists who have taken a natural rather than a moral position; i.e., they assume that drinking behavior and alcoholism can be explained by social and individual forces and not by innate weakness. This school of thought has emphasized the use of the scientific method as a way to learn about and subsequently to teach about alcohol and alcohol problems. However, because no tradition fades easily, even in a rapidly changing society the moralistic approaches are far from dead, and we now have a scientific addition to these traditional beliefs and moralistic notions, not a replacement of them.

Yet the scientific movement is by no means negligible. Representing such physical sciences as biology, physiology, biochemistry, pharmacology, and chemistry and such social sciences as history, law, anthropology, psychology, psychiatry, and sociology, the scientific movement is today sustained and recognized. Various therapy methods for alcoholism have been based on particular scientific notions, and formal organizations have emerged to educate and disseminate the new knowledge.

This new influence of science has a simple overall problem: How can it avoid being absorbed into a revival of the moralistic approach? Two problems seem central in this question. First, the very profusion of efforts from so many different fields of study makes for confusion, resulting in many theories but little agreement. There is a deluge of reports, articles, and research results that are totally unrelated to one another. In some limited sense at least these materials need to be unified for their impact to be felt and for additional testing of their hypotheses. This book represents an effort to integrate some of these scattered materials.

The second problem involved in keeping the scientific rather than the moralistic approach in the forefront grows from the methods of treatment and education generated by the new scientific theories. Operating in an atmosphere of problems and urgency, these activities have rapidly produced private, governmental, and voluntary organizations with budgets, personnel, and techniques for treating alcoholism and educating about alcohol. The big question for the scientific movement is whether or not the therapy and education provided by these organizations, the so-called "alcoholism industry," are effective, and if so, to what degree. Without this type of impersonal assessment, therapies and training may be merely the rituals and ceremonies of a formal organization whereby it perpetuates itself. Although readily available, the principles of evaluation are difficult to put into practice and are apt to be seen as a threat by members of the alcoholism industry. At present practically no objective assessment of their activities is available save for some therapy evaluation. Chapter 7 considers in detail the types of therapies attempted, their success, and the strategy of therapy evaluation as well as the assessment of educational efforts.

THE FUTURE: WHAT ABOUT PREVENTION?

Current signs point to many and probably more alcoholics in the immediate future. As a result, efforts at prevention will come more and more to the fore. Although prevention in the complete meaning of that idealist term seems improbable, some realistic, modest, preventive measures are feasible. Chapter 8 explores and evaluates both those with reasonable prospects and those that appear un-. realistic.

By steady educational pressure the dominant focus of the general population on the late-stage, skid-row type of alcoholic can be diminished. Such efforts may well relocate attention on the early and middle-stage sufferer, who is still a part of stable life. Such a refocusing would, in turn, make way for earlier recognition and treatment and for the association of alcohol pathologies with pivotal institutions such as medicine, industry, and law. Good results in these areas might then prepare the way for reducing the segregation process and the stimulation of effective social controls from "significant others" in the alcoholic's life.

Long-range prevention, however, seems to be quite improbable. To reduce vulnerability to alcoholism calls for sharp changes in cultural values. To assume that the social values of alcohol in American society will decline in the foreseeable future is also unrealistic.

Even though the notion of a "functional substitute" for alcohol—some behavior that would perform the same social functions but expose users to less health risk—is appealing, it seems to have little opportunity to develop.

The strategy of drastically altering the manner in which American children experience alcohol has been suggested. Rather than an adolescent, furtive, ambivalent introduction, some observers believe that a childhood introduction within the controls of family and neighborhood might help to prevent alcoholism. However, it is highly unlikely that the structure and values of American society would change sufficiently to accept this.

THE SOCIAL CLIMATE

The "Wet"-"Dry" Struggle

American society has always shown a sharp ambivalence toward alcohol. Even during the early colonial period moderate use of non-distilled beverages—ales, beers, and wines—was expected and fully approved, but drunkenness, seen as a moral defect indicating weak self-control, was frowned upon and even punished. During the Revolution and postrevolutionary period increased drinking was due to the introduction of high-alcohol-content beverages like rum and whisky;[1] this was coupled with some breakdown in social controls. At the same time, however, there was an underlining of the belief in self-reliance and individual achievement, to which drunkenness was a definite threat. Thus an ambivalent attitude resulted in which alcohol was seen, on the one hand, as a temporary desirable release from relentless reality and, on the other hand, as a major cause of deviation from moral codes and respectable behavior.

One of the major sources of this intense ambiguity lies in the historical clash, which began in the 1830s, between those who pressed for complete prohibition of the manufacture and sale of alcohol, the "drys," and those who wished to drink freely, the "wets." At first the temperance forces relied on persuasion and propagandistic forms of education to point up the dangers of alcohol for individual accomplishment, but as the movement passed into the 1840s their approach grew increasingly militant. The outgrowth of this more aggressive tone was to seek ways to use legislative action rather than moral persuasion in order to ensure sobriety.[2]

From approximately 1890 the prohibitionists, or temperance forces, strained every resource to force Federal prohibition, which, they believed, would be the acme of progress in an achievement-oriented society. According to the drys, to free all Americans from the temptations of liquor would be to free them from an ever-present threat to their self-control, permitting them to achieve their ambitions without constant danger to their will power. Thus the prohibition movement appealed to basic American values, and because it faced little *organized* resistance, the Eighteenth Amendment was passed and ratified in 1917.

Incongruously, millions of Americans continued to drink, and the value of alcohol as a way to enhance the pleasures of social life remained strong. Even the amendment itself and the law to enforce it, the Volstead Act, represented a deep inconsistency, since only manufacture, sale, and transportation of liquor were prohibited, not buying, drinking, or making it at home. Because legal manufacture was suppressed, the stage was set for a decade of illegal manufacture, sale, and transport, which created lawlessness and crime unprecedented in American life.

Thus the opponents of prohibition were able to organize with ample argument. Rather than debate about the possibility for realistic change in the law which might reduce some of the costs of alcohol yet preserve some of its values, the wets sought complete repeal of the Eighteenth Amendment. And they obtained it in 1933, almost fourteen years after its ratification.[3] Now, politically and legally, the country was back where it started.

But was America really back where it started? A society could repeal its laws, but could it repeal the aftereffects of such a battle?

Probably one of the most crippling effects was to wrap any effort to study alcohol objectively in a maze of half-truths and invectives. Neither side had any genuine scientists, but both had many prominent apologists who generated spurious statistics, a practice still used today among many so-called students of alcohol.

The struggle served to embed deeper into American minds the belief that alcohol problems develop because of a drinker's moral weakness or lack of will power. Also rules and procedures for drinking became more irregular and fractured than ever before. The resulting confusion insulated drinking behavior from the social control of such basic institutions as home and church. An excessive drinker came to experience isolation from normal drinkers because "he had lost control of himself," but he could easily find new companions and groups who drank as he did.

The Skid-row Image

The chief damage done by the moral battle to the objective study and treatment of alcoholism was to crystallize a stereotype of the alcoholic as a skid-row bum, sleeping in doorways, parks, and railroad stations, without ties to home or job. With such an image—and its stigma—deeply embedded in American life, a formidable barrier to education and treatment has emerged. Wives cling to the belief that alcoholic husbands "will never get that bad"; bosses, fully aware of a drinking problem in a subordinate, will delay referral to their company's medical department until the chance of treatment is low; general practitioners will fail to diagnose alcoholism because they work from such a stereotype; early-stage alcoholics will refuse to try the program of Alcoholics Anonymous because they believe "I'm not like those guys." Education about early signs of dependent drinking has suffered because millions believe an alcoholic is some kind of skid-row drinker. In reality no more than 5 to 10 percent of the alcoholic population falls in this class, and, as we shall show later, most alcoholics live and work in relatively stable home and job situations spread throughout the community.

Why Drinking Persists in the United States

Because of the moralistic traditions surrounding alcohol, its social costs are well publicized. Investigators proclaim its relationship to highway accidents. Industrialists realize that it is one major cause of absenteeism. Social workers believe that alcohol plays a large role in broken families, and ministers fear it threatens the spiritual life of their congregations. Public health specialists list alcoholism among the most difficult public health problems, and other health problems, such as tuberculosis, are frequently linked with alcohol pathology. In view of its reputation as a problem, why does the drinking of alcohol persist? Our perspective will be greatly aided by an answer to this question.

Foremost among the reasons why Americans drink is the fact that alcohol stimulates sociability. Many people think of it as a social beverage, not as a drug. According to a study by Pfautz, American best-selling novels have increasingly described drinking as a support for social interaction.[4] Authors depict it as a means of creating new social groups as well as a help to sustaining hospitality and good fellowship. Among people who are highly individualistic and who lack basic social skills in relating to others in a genuine way, alcohol acts to reduce barriers and to promote friendliness. The work of Bruun suggests that alcohol may release exuberance and a free flow of conversation, making it easier for persons to get along.[5] It helps fill the need, felt by many, for a satisfying primary-group relationship in a complex society where impersonal, competitive living prevails, and where primary-group life is less evident.[6]

Getting along with people is also important in marital and work life. In young marriages, coming to know one another better, after the social anesthesia of romance has worn off, may be facilitated by alcohol. Also sexual adjustment, as well as emotional adjustment to the frustrations of child rearing, may be aided by moderate, restricted use of alcohol.

In the work world, alcohol facilitates such modern values as establishing rapport with other people, being a part of informal cliques, and being a manipulator. Alcohol offers release from the seriousness and routine of daily life and from the pressures in the working situation to achieve success. In a sense it offers some release from America's less-publicized addiction—"work addiction"— often referred to as "getting ahead in the world."[7]

The foregoing statements lead us to the second major reason why Americans drink: Alcohol is quite effective as a tranquilizer. This fact is confirmed in studies made by Greenberg.[8] American civilization provides few if any organized occasions where release of accumulated tension can take place. Many drinking situations and drinking groups aid in releasing such tension through increased talking, singing, and dancing. No less a luminary than Sigmund Freud believed that moderate use of liquor helped many harassed persons who could not otherwise compensate.[9] Unfortunately, the extreme problem focus on alcohol has so far prevented research from testing the notion that its use may aid mental health for many Americans.

Though not unique to the United States, these positive reasons for drinking are certainly enforced by certain features of American life: individualism, urban anonymity, competitive striving to accomplish, vast differences in social and cultural backgrounds, and the lack of organized occasions for release of tension.

Drinking Groups

Numerous kinds of drinking-centered groups and situations honeycomb recreation, home, and work life in the United States. Taverns, which are present forms of the old saloon and "speakeasy," rank among the most-frequented recreation outlets. Clinard has estimated that taverns in this country number in the hundreds of thousands.[10] Annually millions of Americans drink some form of alcohol within the tavern's premises. Although taverns are heavily regulated, still denounced, and of many types, tavern drinking groups reflect both the values and costs of alcohol. On the one hand, they provide—

especially for persons in large cities—a primary-group relationship facilitating social participation, emotional ties, and in-group loyalties for regular customers. On the other hand, developing alcoholics do a substantial amount of their excessive drinking in taverns where, according to Clinard, they probably find protection, acceptance, and often prestige.[11]

Another type of drinking is done in the home. Most studies show that this type predominates over tavern and bar drinking. Keller states that the sale of beer for home use has steadily overtaken its sales in public drinking places.[12] Although exact figures are lacking, it seems possible that the amount of distilled spirits sold for private home use equals that sold across the bar.

We also lack precise studies of how this home drinking takes place, but probably part of it is casual. It occurs as an accompaniment to family conversation, meals, parental conferences, or informal "neighboring." Still other home drinking is associated with more formal parties. Such serving of alcohol ranges from the cocktail party, with a time limit, to the party where liquor, food, conversation, dancing, and entertainment are all available for long periods of time. These can be termed "drinking-centered parties," where food is apt to be secondary. Of course a family might give a cocktail party outside the family domain. Outside-the-home parties occur in many restaurants, bars, night clubs, and private clubs. Here drinking and dancing are the chief recreation, but "letting go" is avoided. A larksome atmosphere often prevails, in which alcohol serves to blur the tension and humdrum of everyday living. Much dating and courtship falls within such a drinking pattern.

Ceremonials such as weddings, graduations, retirements, class reunions, and holidays precipitate a lot of the drinking done in America. The participants in such group ceremonials associate alcohol with the ceremony, the emotion, and the symbolism of the occasion.

Alcohol is also a prominent part of professional society meetings, occupational meetings, union meetings, welfare conferences, and business conclaves. The whole gamut of conventions is replete with alcohol as a part of the affair. Often the main items of business take place over a drink in a nearby hotel cocktail lounge or bar. Renewal of friendships, making of new ones, and general fraternizing often include drinking as part of the exchange.

At the same time, however, roughly one-third of the population of the United States of typical drinking age are teetotalers. Usually they oppose drinking on moral grounds. Compared with drinkers, they are a minority, somewhat older, usually of rural background, of abstemious parents, and of strong religious beliefs that define all drinking as sinful. They represent the norm of complete abstinence as a way to define alcohol's effects. A study of abstainers in California shows some evidence of them as socializing much less than drinkers.[13] This group identifies alcohol with divorce, poverty, and crime. They see little, if any, good in drinking. Although the Protestant ethic of self-denial, hard work, and suspicion of emotion is believed to be dead, it is apparently much alive in this sizable part of America's population. Though, according to Keller, the number of abstainers has dropped in the past three generations[14] from probably as much as 60 percent of the adult population, the conflict over alcohol and its value is still much alive in modern America.

Those who drink in some quantity and frequency include the cost of alcohol as a regular part of family budgets. In 1960 Americans spent 3 percent of their total personal outlay on alcoholic beverages. In 1950 the figure was 4.1 percent. McCarthy has explained in a study of consumer expenditures for alcoholic beverages that during this time the total outlay for commercial recreation rose slightly.[15] The period also saw a continuance of the sharp trend toward the use of beer. The absolute amount of alcohol drunk in beer, during this period, exceeded that consumed from distilled beverages. This unusual trend began in the mid-thirties, following repeal of prohibition, and by 1960 was a dramatic shift. In per capita terms, the decade between 1950 and 1960 saw a leveling off of absolute alcohol consumed at about 2 gallons for persons fifteen years of age and over. This per capita rate is noticeably less than during decades before and immediately after the turn of the century.

Roughly 15 to 20 percent of those in the legal drinking ages drink regularly. Somewhat over half do so occasionally. The remainder are abstainers. Approximately 5 percent are problem drinkers or alcoholics. Regular drinkers consume relatively large amounts when they drink. Those who drink occasionally do so only two or three times per month with only one or two drinks per sitting. These facts have become apparent through various quantity-frequency studies in the states of Washington, California, and Iowa.[16]

Age and Sex

When we consider various age groups, we find that the percentage of drinkers becomes less as the group increases in age. Also, those who do drink tend to drink less. Some studies place the highest percentage of users in the eighteen- to twenty-one-year age category, while others find it somewhat higher. To a degree, then, regular use is related to young adulthood. This probably reflects social changes in America, whereby drinking has become more respectable for younger generations. Also, as one gets older, pressures of home or work replace recreation related to drinking. Greater disapproval of drinking may appear with age because of religious and health concerns.

In contrast, older children and adolescents drink alcohol infrequently and in small amounts. Although, according to Straus, about half of the childhood population has experienced alcohol in some form by the age ten,[17] its use is not a typical childhood experience by any means. As late adolescence and young adulthood occur, the probability of being a user goes up sharply. Apparently the use of alcohol is a symbol of approaching adulthood. Maddox in writing about adolescence and alcohol states that many adolescents seem to use alcohol as a help in resolving the question, "When am I an adult?"[18] After attaining adulthood, however, most young people find drinking less meaningful as a status symbol.

The quantity and frequency of drinking are related to the sex of the drinker. Throughout a great deal of American history, drinking has been chiefly a male practice. Consistently, in study after study, significantly more males than females are drinkers. Consistently, more men than women are regular and heavy users of alcohol. According to Keller, the sexes are roughly equal among occasional drinkers, but males drink more and they drink more often.[19] Men also tend less to be total abstainers but tend to drink more regularly throughout the week than on weekends and to drink more in taverns, bars, and private clubs. Women, in contrast, drink more at home. Earlier in this century, these sex differences were more pronounced than they are today. Recent studies conclude that currently the trend is toward less sex difference, especially in higher social classes. This reflects the changing roles of women in modern America.

It is doubtful, however, that similar drinking patterns for the sexes will emerge any time in the near future. Ullman concludes that even though the general increase in the number of people who drink is due, in part, to more women participating, other, more basic factors operate to reduce female drinking.[20] Women in the lower middle class tend to show strong disapproval of drinking. Probably more influential, however, is the fact that women typically learn a drinking style that goes along with being female. Rather than showing prowess by drinking, they learn to show caution and shyness by light imbibing. The value placed on sexual purity remains potent despite some weakening influences. Women learn that alcohol's release of inhibitions might lead them to violate sex taboos. There seems to be almost universal social pressure against unrestrained drinking by women, and a general intolerance of drunken women exists at all levels.

This is not so for the American male. Regardless of social class, young males frequently respond to counsels such as "Drink like a man" or "Hold your liquor." Instead of pressures to drink cautiously, they find cultural cues to use and abuse alcohol to show power, a venturesome spirit, and freedom of action. This may be due, in part, to less sexual danger for intoxicated males than for females.

Social Class

Another variable influencing American drinking patterns is social class. Typical indexes of social strata are education, occupation, and income. Very little is known about specific occupational differences and drinking, but Riley and Marden have concluded that as education and income rise (with the exception of young males) there is a steady rise in the number of drinkers and the frequency of drinking, especially among urban people.[21] Gusfield has shown that upper socioeconomic groups are more permissive in their drinking habits than are lower-status groups.[22] Also the higher strata express their wealth in more expensive drinking patterns. The cocktail party and similar events are more characteristic of middle- and upper-class groups, while tavern drinking is engaged in more by the lower-class groups. As education and income rise, there is less difference between the numbers of male and female drinkers. According to Mulford and Miller, at lower-status levels, Methodists are far more abstemious than are Catholics, but this difference tends to decrease as education rises.[23] Thus social class seems to cancel differences in drinking behavior between social groups, regardless of sex or religion.

Differences in drinking patterns of various social strata might be explained by examining the past. In the early nineteenth century, changes in the social makeup of the American middle class created a shift from a belief in complete abstinence to a tolerance of drinking. Professionals, independent farmers, and small businessmen, who constituted the backbone · of the temperance movement, gave way to large-scale urban-centered organizations. From these emerged a new middle class made up of salaried, managerial, and white-collar personnel. For these Americans, ability to get along and to be tolerant became important. Gusfield believes that drinking fitted into such social values because it helped to reduce inhibitions and promoted friendliness.[24] Rather than being religious about the old-fashioned notion of sin, these middle- and upper-class groups sought through a distinctive style of drinking to be fashionable and different from lower-status groups. These social values, plus the fact that the higher social strata enjoyed a freedom from close supervision on the job and a more tolerant treatment from police, combined to suggest a higher rate of drinkers and drinking in the higher social classes.

Rural-Urban Differences

Studies of rural-urban drinking patterns show another set of differences. Popham found that farm and small-village areas have fewer drinkers and less heavy drinking than do urban, industrialized areas.[25] As rural-reared persons migrate to urban areas, however, the number of drinkers among them, as well as the frequency of use, tend to go up. Probably this pattern reflects the strong influence in rural areas of ascetic Protestantism, a belief that indulgence of the senses is bad and that alcohol promotes sensualism.

Racial, Ethnic, and Religious Differences

Finally, racial, religious, and ethnic groups show differences in quantity and frequency of drinking. Unfortunately we know very little about the Negroes, who rank just below the Caucasoids as the largest racial group in American life. Indirect evidence suggests that the Negro middle class identifies with the Protestant ethic that to drink is to give in to impulse. Maddox and Jennings have shown us, however, that the Negro's tremendous sense of inferiority makes alcohol's ability to change reality especially attractive.[26] Therefore many middle-class Negroes drink, often excessively, but with a very strong sense of loss of self-control. About specific quantity and frequency of drinking we know practically nothing. On the other hand, the rate of alcoholism is as high among Negroes as among the white population; it is possibly higher.

Italian-Americans have drinking customs quite in contrast to those of native Americans. These immigrants have been influenced by the drinking habits of their native country, where wine is drunk exclusively with meals and is looked upon with casual indifference as simply a part of living.[27] In Italy drunkenness is frowned upon as regular individual behavior even at festive occasions. Alcohol problems are almost nonexistent in Italy. Thus in Italian-American groups, though changes toward American-type drinking have occurred (in addition to wine they drink beer and distilled spirits and drink at times other than mealtimes) and have caused an increase in alcohol problems, these problems are still negligible compared with those among native Americans.[28]

As we have noted earlier, Jewish-Americans, especially the Orthodox, have an unusual drinking pattern. Alcohol is part of their religious ritual. Like Italians they drink early in childhood, and practically all adults are regular drinkers. Yet, as Snyder shows, practically none are alcoholic.[29] Used in a sanctified way, alcohol rests at the very core of family and religious controls, but uncontrolled drinking and drunkenness is abominable to the Orthodox Jew. Though the influence of this pattern of drinking is felt in the Reformed and Conservative groups, their alcohol problems increase as they assimilate American values. In Chapter 4 we shall see cases of Orthodox Jewish alcoholics who represent this breakup of traditional values.

Barnett has studied the Cantonese Chinese, another ethnic group within which drinking takes place under regulated circumstances.[30] As in the Italian and Jewish groups, drinking among the Cantonese Chinese is a part of childhood behavior, of ceremonial festivities and family meals, and includes the use of a great deal of wine. Also, as in the other two ethnic groups, there is a consistent permissive attitude toward drinking, but a forbidding one toward drunkenness. Drinking problems are few, and practically no alcoholism is found among those directly participating in the subculture.

We might summarize the drinking patterns of the Italian-American, Jew, and Chinese by saying that each shows the influence of group controls when the drinker remains within the confines of the group. The norms of the group regulate how to drink, and deviation is effectively controlled. Unlike the pattern in American society generally, the drinker is surrounded by clear negative sanctions. He is not rejected and isolated but is brought under the social controls of the group.

In contrast to the Italian-American, Jewish, and Chinese drinking patterns, the habits of the Irish-Americans engender a disproportionately large number of alcohol problems. Reflecting native Irish customs, they drink distilled spirits, mainly whisky, and accept heavy drinking as normal. Migration to America reinforced their pattern. Glad has observed that many Irish-American males are heavy drinkers, and the typical norm is utilitarian: Drink to get the physical and psychological changes brought on by alcohol.[31] But conflicting attitudes toward drinking exist. There is no strong disapproval of drunkenness, yet parents restrict their children's drinking because they have seen many alcohol problems. Children learn about alcohol under unregulated conditions outside the home. Ullman believes that because "Drink like a man" is a familiar pressure to the Irish-American, the youths tend to become intoxicated in even early drinking experiences.[32]

Two religious groupings, the Methodist and Mormon churches, represent the total abstinent view toward alcohol and thus are at variance with the social milieu of American life. Despite the Methodist church's official position of total abstinence, however, there are, as Hooten has revealed, definite signs of change,[33] and many Methodists do drink. Skolnick has shown that Methodist young people often learn about alcohol outside the home (even if the parents drink) and imbibe with the disapproval of their parents,[34] but there is little evidence of marked drinking problems.

Among Mormons who drink, however, alcohol problems are relatively frequent.[35] These conclusions were drawn from a comprehensive study of college students from various religious groups. To the Mormon church there is only one rule—abstinence. Apparently those who do drink learn from nonmembers or deviant members and experience no defining controls from their home or church.

Comparison with Other Societies

In the United States we do not have a uniform drinking custom. Drinking behavior remains many things for many people. Variances in age, sex, social class, ethnic and religious groups, and rural versus urban living make for differences in drinking according to quantity, frequency, and social meaning. Nor do we have uniform social sanctions. Perhaps customs and sanctions are slowly evolving, but currently they are not highly visible. And, unlike Italy, where clear traditions control drinking behavior, the United States has a high incidence of alcohol problems.

France, on the other hand, has a very consistent and widely accepted drinking custom, but it also has a high incidence of alcohol pathologies. According to Jellinek, alcohol in near-intoxicating amounts is regularly in the bloodstreams of many French workers most of the day and evening. Most of these people do not become obviously drunk, but the continuous presence of alcohol in their systems leads to a high tissue tolerance which, in turn, leads to even heavier wine drinking. Jellinek has classified this type of alcoholism as "Delta" alcoholism. Physiological symptoms such as increased tissue tolerance and withdrawal symptoms do occur, but the intense psychological misery and social rejections do not take place as they do in the Gamma type of alcoholism predominant in America.[36] The reason for this is that for French people intoxication is not an intermittent behavior but a daily, regular matter in no way laden with guilt as it probably would be for most Americans. The French people accept heavy wine drinking as not only desirable and healthy but socially necessary. Whereas the Italian attitude toward the abstainer is one of indifference, the nondrinker in France meets with ridicule and contempt. Apparently in modern, complex societies exposure to heavy drinking, regardless of uniform social customs, seems to increase alcohol problems. These problems may differ in kind as between the United States and France, but they are alcohol pathologies nonetheless.

Turning to preliterate cultures, we find that the Camba of eastern Bolivia provide a rather clear contrast to drinking behavior in America. The Camba peasant tenant farmers live in small nuclear families isolated from one another. Social activities are almost nonexistent in this culture except for frequent *fiestas*. At this time the people congregate in village streets or houses in small groups to drink a distilled cane liquor of high alcohol content. As Heath relates in a study of the Camba drinking patterns, often the *fiestas* last two or three days, and informal groups of drinkers will drink steadily during the entire period.[37] No aggression or sexual deviation occurs. No drinker is rejected for his behavior. Children are excluded from the drinking, but they perform chores such as carrying away empty bottles and going to the sellers for new bottles. Apparently the Camba never drink except during these *fiesta* periods, and solitary drinking is unthinkable. According to Heath, alcoholism, as we know it in America, does not exist. The Camba have no fear of the results of drinking alcohol, no hangovers, no guilt, and experience no harmful effects on their work.

In contrast to the situation in American society, social values of the Camba provide a base for acceptance rather than rejection of drinking and drunkenness. Even if a Camba drinker should be rejected, he could find no other group to drink with. In the United States, however, after rejection by one drinking group, a drinker has many opportunities to find tolerant companions.

Studies made of other preliterate groups, the Mohave Indians, the Indians who inhabit the Northwest in North America, and the Andean Indians, reveal that with even minor ambivalence toward drinking alcohol, no types of alcoholism exist.[38] These Indians recognize the value of alcohol as a way to lessen inner strain and to promote integration and strong bonds within the tribe. Though they show some mild concern about the results of heavy drinking, getting drunk is not reprehensible, and no guilt feelings result.

According to a study by Lemert among Polynesians, systematic stigma is rare, and no guilt develops from drunkenness, yet drunken behavior threatens the strong Polynesian social values of acceptance and recognition by friends and associates.[39] There is no opportunity, however, to move into a well-organized deviant drinking group, and it is unheard of to "go it alone." Hence, even though ambivalence toward drinking alcohol does exist, alcohol pathologies are not increased.

With both literate and simple societies as a background, what can we say about American society? We have already noted the long-standing confusion and lack of uniform values concerning alcohol.

Though this comparatively great ambivalence is not enough in itself to foster alcoholism, it sets the stage for the isolation of the excessive drinker, and it weakens social controls. Why does the excessive drinker steadily become isolated? Both he and his associates esteem the social value of will power, believing that he should be able to drink without becoming too intoxicated. When he repeatedly cannot do this, he and his peers become disgusted. American society slowly assigns to the regularly drunken person the role of a pariah, exiling him and thus further encouraging him to become an alcoholic. Along the way there is a peculiar intermingling of reward and punishment but no clear negative sanctions that regulate and define how to drink.

WHAT IS ALCOHOLISM?

We can reach a definition of alcoholism in two ways: (1) by focusing on the way recurrent use of alcohol disrupts role performance, and (2) by tracing "alcoholism progression," i.e., the typical symptoms that characterize the disorder. The first is more practical, more general, and more easily communicated. The latter is more clinical, more technical, and more aimed at spelling out a specific type of alcoholism—that which is predominant in America. For overview, it seems best to start with the first type of definition.

Role-impairment Definition

Four facets of behavior set the alcoholic apart from his surrounding fellow drinkers. First, his use of alcohol regularly deviates from the typical drinking standards of his key social groups—home, neighborhood, and job. Second, the performance of his role in these key institutions is impaired. Third, he suffers emotional and physical damage from his regular excessive use of alcohol. Finally, he shows an inability to stop drinking once he starts, even though he knows his drinking impairs his life; thus, his use of alcohol is beyond his conscious control.

The first distinctive feature, deviation from drinking norms, obviously varies from society to society, and in a complex society such as America, from subculture to subculture. Thus alcoholism is a different thing in France from what it is in America. The French, who experience little guilt or stigma with drinking, show physical rather than psychiatric symptoms of alcoholism. The middle-class Protestant American, on the other hand, shows emotional damage from excessive drinking as is evidenced in his guilt feelings, his lying to protect his drinking, and his deep resentment of those around him. Particularly characteristic of the alcoholic in the United States is his inability to control the amount of alcohol consumed. In France the typical alcoholic drinks constantly but does so at a controlled level.

Still, regardless of type, the alcoholic differs from those around him because the performance of his adult roles is clearly impaired by his recurrent use of alcohol. In America most alcoholics are very poor husbands and fathers or wives and mothers, and on the job they rate consistently lower in performance than do other employees. In addition, their unreliable behavior makes for doubts and confusion in intimate friendships.

Not only does alcoholism bring about changes in what others can expect of the sufferer, but it also damages him directly. The impairment of physical health by steady exposure to heavy drinking is evident in liver and nutritional diseases. Recall that the middle-class American may also experience emotional damage. The feeling that his inability to drink as others do indicates lack of will power, plus the accumulated social pressure to be relentlessly self-reliant, repeatedly hurt his own image of himself. He will curse his behavior and try again to drink as others do, only to find he cannot. Then, to protect his deviant drinking, he will lie in every conceivable manner and rationalize to the extreme.

Finally, the alcoholic differs, especially in America, in that once he begins to drink, a reaction occurs wherein he experiences a deep need for alcohol. Because he cannot regulate the quantity he will consume, his drinking may last hours, days, or weeks and continue to the point of his being either too intoxicated or too sick to drink more. Whether or not this compulsion to drink is physiological, a self-fulfilling prophecy, or possibly hysteria is a wide open question.

Equally hard to answer is why the alcoholic begins to drink again after a fairly long period of sobriety during which he is back to good health and is reaccepted at home and at work. His relapse is a puzzle to everyone including himself. Apparently the alcoholic believes that under normal social pressures to drink he can find the will power to set a limit on how much he consumes. Yet he cannot, and the more he tries, the more he loses what little control he had.

There are several factors involved in the relapse to drinking. Alcohol helps the alcoholic to satisfy some of his most basic psychological needs. It does more for him than just relax his tensions and anxieties. Through alcohol he can receive certain emotional responses from drinking associates which make him feel worthy, independent, sought after, and loved, thus satisfying his unusually great need for security, response, or recognition. In addition, alcohol may well provide the drinker with an exquisite chance for new experience by helping him to revolt against undesirable restrictions. In other words, he can shed adult responsibilities of work and family. Relapse, then, often represents a return to a desirable state even though awful hangover and embarrassing loss of control may result. The rewards a drinker gets from relapse may more than make up for weak and confused social punishments and threats.

Alcoholism Progression: Early Symptoms

Jellinek has divided various phases of alcoholism into an early stage, a middle stage, and a late stage.[1] Though it is difficult to determine where regular social drinking ends and early-stage alcoholism begins, the early symptoms of alcoholism do offer a clue.

These early symptoms of the American type of alcoholism are so intertwined with various forms of drinking that they go practically unnoticed by even close friends and drinking companions. The best example of a symptom which is not obvious to others but is felt internally and subjectively by the developing alcoholic is the "blackout," often referred to as "pulling a blank." The term means that a drinker cannot remember what happened during a drinking session even though during that time he continued to act in the expected manner. If he "blacks out" at a ball game, he may continue to cheer, comment, and otherwise behave as others around him, but the following day he cannot remember what happened. A temporary amnesia has accompanied his drinking. Such blackouts are different from "passing out," where the drinker loses conscious control of his muscular system and is immobile, as in sleep.

Occasional blackouts and passouts happen to the ordinary drinker, but recurrent blackouts during drinking episodes are one of the earliest signs of alcoholism. They accompany and reflect a definite increase in *tolerance* for alcohol: Steadily the developing alcoholic must drink more to get the same subjective "glow." Whereas before, two martinis had produced a feeling of well-being and gregarious friendship, now three or four are required. This increased drinking because of increased tolerance is a second early sign of alcoholism, and can be a source of social recognition. Unfortunately, prestige comes to many, especially young males, if their tolerance for alcohol is high. In much the same way blackouts have prestige value in some drinking groups.

The practice of sneaking drinks indicates the extent to which the developing alcoholic deviates from those around him. In a secretive way he manages to drink more per occasion than others by drinking faster without being obvious, by furtively leaving his friends and getting a drink, by fortifying himself well in advance of a drinking situation, or by helping out as bartender in order to be close to the supply. These actions indicate his overconcern for enough alcohol to meet his growing needs.

Even in these early stages, the alcoholic senses his difference from others and feels guilty about it. As this sensitivity increases, he forms all sorts of reasons for his drinking, and, at the same time, encourages others to "drink up" so that his heavy drinking will not be conspicuous. All these stratagems serve to delude him into believing his drinking is normal in order to blot out his growing feeling of guilt.

During this early stage the developing alcoholic continues to work, to perform his family duties, and even to improve in some part of these key roles. He covers up intermittent but severe ruptures in his family and work life with renewed efforts that make up for the lapse. As yet he is not an uncontrolled drinker, but more and more he is relying on alcohol as *the* way to adjust. Reinforced by the social rewards for drinking, alcohol is rapidly coming to be his chief method of coping with tensions and anxieties.

Middle-phase Symptoms

With loss of control, however, the developing alcoholic moves into the middle phase of his illness. At this point his drinking regularly disrupts his performance on the job through growing absenteeism[2] and at home, where normal family life deteriorates. Yet the change is slow and insidious with no specific day or month marking the development of uncontrolled drinking.

Oddly enough, the more the drinker loses control, the more he insists he can stop if he really wants to. He goes on the wagon for a definite period in order to prove to himself and those growing concerned about him that he can control his drinking if he decides to do so. Without this reassurance, his blackouts, loss of control, and preoccupation with alcohol begin to damage his self-image, and somehow he must protect his view of himself from the truth.

Another way to protect this self-image is to protect his job as much as possible from the influence of his alcoholism. At work he uses up a lot of his ability just trying to appear normal. As we shall see in Chapter 5, if he is a manual laborer he goes to great lengths to avoid on-the-job accidents which would bring him under very close scrutiny. His extra precautions reduce the amount of work done but ensure that it is done safely. If he is a white-collar or salaried worker, he will try to avoid absenteeism if at all possible. Though absences will soon increase and then become abnormal, at first the drinker will make every attempt to stay on the job. This going to work, regardless of how awful he feels, is his way of denying that there is anything unusual or different about his use of alcohol.[3]

Going to work also helps to lessen the tremendous sense of guilt present among high-status professional and managerial employees who drink excessively. Backed up by an ingrained sense of duty, they believe something is very wrong in their permitting their drinking to interfere with going to the job.

Later, as loss of control becomes more complete and the drinker, regardless of occupation, becomes more visible to others, he resorts to precautions, lies, excuses, and other guilt reducers. He may avoid talk that would lead to his admission of drunkenness or of having a hangover, and he may try drinking with new drinking associates. Still his close friends, boss, and family know of his problem and urge him to slow down. So, despite his armor of rationalizations, his guilt and self-hate increase.

In response to these guilt feelings, the problem drinker begins to work in a frenzy for a time, only to slump off into poor work again. During the frenzy he attempts to do more than he can actually accomplish, but in the mania of effort he reduces the self-hate. Periods of making up to family and friends, including almost impossible promises and schemes, go along with this effort to reestablish self-esteem. During this time of trying to justify his behavior on the one hand and regain control of his drinking on the other, he may also blame others for pressuring him, misunderstanding him, and driving him to drink.

Efforts to recapture control at this stage can be varied and ingenious. According to Jellinek, the developing alcoholic in striving to regain control tries times when he can drink and when he must not. He changes types of liquor, ways of mixing it, and speeds of drinking. He sets up rules about where he can drink and how much in each place. Some of these actions deceive him into believing he really is controlling how much he drinks.[4]

Actually he is merely losing control in a different way, or in different surroundings, for now he has come to be openly intoxicated in many situations. Despite his resolve to confine and regulate, he has succeeded in increasing the accepted drinking times and occasions, not reducing them. Drinking has come to be central in his life, and he spends a majority of his waking hours planning and managing his drinking. Rather than thinking that drinking disrupts his job or home life, he has come to reverse the concern and to wonder if the demands of particular roles will disrupt his drinking.

Now, in this middle phase, he must manage far more than family complaints, employer suspicions, and the advice of well-meaning friends. A triple threat faces him—supply, hangovers, and eating. As he undergoes closer surveillance and more social pressures, the problem of having a ready supply of liquor mounts and becomes close to an obsession.

With the hiding of his supply, the alcoholic deviates completely. This action signals a point where he has become so determined to avoid notice that he tries to deceive everyone in his life as well as himself. And for a time he succeeds, but only partly. His withdrawal and his different behavior is noticed by his fellow workers, his spouse, his close friends, and his boss. Because, however, the alcoholic is able to have some sober periods, realization by the key people in his life of what is happening is a jerky process. During such periods the drinker can convince these key people that he is controlling himself.

It is here that we can see the emergence of a major dimension of societal response to deviance: The key people in the alcoholic's life vacillate, absorb, and hesitate, giving him an opportunity to continue his inexorable march toward the late stage. Since knowledge about alcoholism is not widespread even today, these key people fail to think of the drinker as being ill. Slowly they will come to reject him and he them; but, for a crucial time, he receives the sometimes hopeful, sometimes grudging help and tolerance from the "significant others" in his life. When these others finally do attempt to apply sanctions, it is usually too late, and the sanctions are too feeble and too irregular. At a time when consistently applied controls (wife could leave, boss could tell him simply and clearly why his work is poor) could define his drinking as a problem and sharply discourage it by decisive action, the wife or boss vacillates, reflecting the traditionally American ambiguous feelings about alcohol. Desperately the alcoholic devises ways to manipulate them into further indecision, and so he progresses further into the middle stages.

The hangover now becomes awful. No longer is it the mild physical imbalance of the regular social drinker. Now it looms as a harsh torment to be avoided if at all possible. Its frightfulness parallels the withdrawal agony of opiate addiction. Thirst, nausea, headache, fatigue, tremors, and self-hate become magnified to gigantic and terrifying sizes. Nausea often becomes "dry heaves," a violent wretching with no results. Tremors become uncontrollable shakes, making the victim unable to hold a coffee cup steady. Fatigue borders on physical collapse. Latent physical illnesses, such as liver and heart disease, may become aggravated by severe hangover.

The most excruciating pain, however, is emotional. The guilt of having lost again, the hopelessness this loss reinforces, the anxiety about the future, and the remorse and utter despair are unbearable. Compared with the physical misery, this psychic pain looms much larger. At its center lies the stark hate of self, arising from failing to live up to the potent social value of self-control. Underscoring and aggravating these feelings of self-hate are expanded blackouts. Typically they have come to cover longer and longer periods of time, leaving the hungover alcoholic with the wildest fears about what he might have done but which he cannot remember.

So withdrawal distress must be managed. Threatening emotions and physical agony of hangover can be anesthetized by more liquor. Now the last shred of "normal" drinking, avoiding the morning period, is abandoned by the alcoholic. To reenter the peace and rewards of intoxication, he drinks any time—morning, noon, or any hour.

In addition he forgets to eat. Alcohol helps him do this. Even though a poor food, it gives him immediate energy. Deeply preoccupied with his drinking, he finds food unimportant. In these two symptoms—morning drinking and poor eating—the alcoholic sets the stage for a chronic illness. Prior to this time his loss of control had so expressed itself that nighttime interferences of some kind would intervene. For example, his drinking would be terminated by going to sleep or passing out. Now, however, the hangover accelerates loss of control. He may start to "come out of it" dimly in the morning only to drink immediately as a way to avoid hangover agony and as a substitute for breakfast. This may enable him to go through the motions of an ordinary workday looking somewhat normal, but once he starts drinking his dependence has increased so that it becomes an around-the-clock matter.

Late-stage Symptoms

As these symptoms repeat and intensify over years of drinking, the alcoholic approaches the late stage. Most alcoholics spend most of their time in the early and middle stages; but because the late stages are spectacular and often bizarre, alcoholism is popularly thought of in late-stage terms. Novels and movies about alcoholics focus on the "lost weekend" symptoms. Welfare concern for the skid-row alcoholic adds to this stereotype of the alcoholic in America. In technical parlance, the late period is the chronic one. Symptoms become deeply exaggerated and impairment almost total.

A fear, almost impossible to describe, of being trapped without a supply of liquor comes to haunt the alcoholic. He literally goes to all lengths to avoid such a frightful condition. His singleness of purpose shows the depth and completeness of his obsession. Hangovers are almost instantly drowned in more liquor. This leads to long periods of drunkenness or near drunkenness. For many alcoholics such periods become "binges" in which drinking occurs in total disregard of time of day or week, of duties and responsibilities, or of financial investment.

However, the alcoholic still manages some periods of sobriety. Tremulous, nervous, pale, and rigid, he musters some hidden reservoir of energy and "goes on the wagon." More frequently he manages to appear sober when actually he has imbibed heavily. Secret, solitary drinking has primed him to look somewhat normal.

Ironically, he is controlling alcoholism with alcohol and using its immediate effects to cope with the overt or obvious signs of complete addiction. Probably he uses alcohol to prepare for any appearance. For example, to shave requires some steadiness, or to put on makeup requires hand precision, and without some alcohol he probably cannot even perform these acts.

The alcoholic becomes completely and absolutely dependent upon alcohol. Even to get out of bed, to avoid the dizziness, the all-consuming nausea, and the uncontrollable shakes require alcohol. At this stage he may find it impossible to keep a drink down without trying three or four times. Just to get the relief of one drink may require hours of crawling, vomiting, of trying to get liquor to the mouth. But to be without it is a form of horrible death. When the alcoholic cannot get alcohol, he engages in, on the one hand, the most pitiful and fantastic effort to secure a supply, and, on the other hand, a determined, calculated quest that borders on the superhuman. Nothing is sacred if it can be exchanged for alcohol. But once the liquor is in hand all seems right with the world.

Often, just about anything with alcohol in it will suffice—vanilla extract, shaving lotion, and even "canned heat," a form of methyl alcohol far more toxic than ethyl alcohol. Since eating is nearly nonexistent, diseases of malnutrition, such as pellagra, beriberi, and scurvy, are frequent. A form of mild paralysis, polyneuritis, also results from severe vitamin deficiency. Muscular pain, followed by inability to operate feet, legs, or arms, are its main symptoms.

Less common are alcoholic psychoses. Nonetheless, delirium tremens is a substantial risk. "D.t.'s" is a severe psychotic condition producing terrifying hallucinations. Often the drinker sees large numbers of small objects suffocating, eating, or pursuing him. Some alcoholics have described the visions as thousands of tiny buttons filling the entire room; millions of ants massing on the bed, engulfing him; or innumerable worms wiggling toward him. Others constantly see and hear some terrifying threat—a huge bird hovering just above or some gigantic rabbit appearing and reappearing seemingly prepared to nibble and feast on the sufferer. Such debilitating visions can last from three to seven or eight days. Fortunately current treatment methods have reduced the fatalities during this period. Death still occurs, however, in a number of cases—up to 15 percent.

Other psychoses can occur. A completely disorganizing memory lapse can produce hospitalization for years. Korsakoff's psychosis, as it is known, leaves the alcoholic without a memory sequence. He can recall only fragments and tends to fill in the gaps by imagination or delusion. Other psychoses are rare but always a possibility. Beyond the faintest doubt, the alcoholic is truly a sick person—physically and emotionally. He desperately requires treatment, hospitalization, and some kind of emergency aid when in the acute periods of late-stage alcoholism.

It is during this late stage that the reaction of those around him crystallizes. For months or years he has been moving toward isolation from his friends and relatives. At this point, however, the alcoholic is fully stigmatized, rejected, and labeled. The wife finally gives up; the company provides its last chance; and hospitals, doctors, ministers, priests, and lawyers shun him. He becomes a pariah, a true deviant. The peculiar intermingling of rewards and punishments has been finally resolved. After years of indecision, society decides that the alcoholic is unfit for inclusion and comes to a point of total rejection.

Trice and Wohl show that the progression of alcoholism to this point moves forward as syndromes, not as individual symptoms.[5] In the early stages blackouts and regular intoxication combine with increased tolerance to form a cluster of symptoms. Loss of control, protecting supply, and morning drinking form a group of symptoms moving toward middle-stage alcoholism. Finally convulsions, nutritional diseases, and severe hangover signal late stages. Sprinkled among and attached to these clusters are numerous other single symptoms and signs forming a complex physical and emotional disorder.

Regardless of which one of the two definitions of alcoholism you use, the term "sick" or "ill" seems fully justified. Job and family roles are impaired from middle symptoms on, and, as we have just seen, a natural history of symptoms indicates an illness in the technical sense of that word.[6] The moralistic tradition about alcohol, however, colors public definitions. Despite well-organized, sustained educational efforts by natural and local health groups, many Americans still believe alcoholics are morally weak, not sick.[7] However, a sizable part of the general population uses *only* the "sick" label.

Probably the main reaction is a mixed one. Reflecting the social confusion about alcohol itself, most Americans believe the alcoholic is both morally weak and truly sick. As one boss said of an alcoholic employee, "He's sick all right, but from something he could have prevented by his own will power."

Prevalence and Distribution of Alcoholism

The most obvious aspect of alcohol as a social problem is reflected in the approximately 4,500,000 Americans in some stage of alcoholism in 1960. This mere fact of numbers makes alcoholism a first-order health problem. There is no evidence, however, that the percentage of alcoholics has increased. Keller estimates that the rate of chronic alcoholism was nearly twice as high in 1910 as in 1955.[8] Careful estimates also show no rate increase in the post–World War II period. It seems reasonable to assume that alcoholism rates have stayed rather constant in the United States in the past twenty-five years. Naturally, as the population has increased, alcoholism has risen proportionately, but the percentage of alcoholics in the total population appears to have remained the same.

The decline of overall rates over decades, however, does not lessen the social damage of the malady. According to the best estimates, there are 3,760,000 men and 710,000 women alcoholics. Not only are they predominantly male, but they are concentrated in the productive years of thirty-five to fifty, adding to the magnitude of the problem. Unlike the effect of opiate addiction, the impact of alcoholism is felt throughout the many social strata of American society and within its pivotal institutions. The old-line, stable professions feel its influence: Doctors face the problem of treating a widespread illness; judges must deal with it in police courts, divorce proceedings, and certain forms of crime. Wellman and Maxwell have shown that high, middle, and low classes all have a sizable number of alcoholics.[9] The evidence permits only a general statement, but it does tell us that the skid-row alcoholic is most unrepresentative of alcoholics in America.

Other research by Straus and Bacon shows that many of these addicted persons are more stable than has been previously believed.[10] In marital, job, and residential terms, many alcoholics continue to be more like the general population than like fellow alcoholics admitted to state hospitals or confined in jails. Middle-stage alcoholics, of the middle and upper classes, because of their comparative stability and because "significant others" absorb their behavior and vacillate about taking firm action, are relatively invisible and do not run high risks of being arrested or committed to state hospitals. Although their job and family roles have been sharply damaged, these alcoholics go unrecognized and tolerated. Also a number of late-stage alcoholics in the middle and upper classes remain shielded from diagnosis because they enjoy more privacy and freedom from job supervision.

In sum, higher-status alcoholics appear less in official statistics because their style of drinking seems to be less open to public view and more covered up by the alcoholic himself.[11] Lower-class alcoholics, on the other hand, seem more inclined to drink openly, exposing their loss of control in taverns, among work associates, and to police. Combined with closer job supervision, which exposes their drinking problem, is the fact that they become more visible and are more apt to become a "statistic" in some public hospital, jail, or court.

Alcoholics show a clustering in urban rather than rural areas. Studies by Seeley, in both Canada and the United States, show that the more urban a state or province, the higher the prevalence of alcoholism.[12] The value of alcohol seems to be enhanced by urban living, leading to more users and to heavier use. This, in turn, exposes susceptible people to alcoholism. Rural areas contain the greater number of leftovers of the "dry" sentiment, ruling out alcohol as a way to cope with tension and emotional needs. We should be aware, however, that rural-urban differences may be due to underreporting in rural areas and more accurate reports in large towns and cities. In rural sections, concern about the social stigma of a patient may prevent physicians from labeling a person an alcoholic. Also, one of the indexes used to estimate the prevalence of alcoholism—cirrhosis of the liver—may often be missed unless an autopsy is performed—an action taken less in small towns than in urban areas.

More certainty attaches to the tendency for alcoholics to come from certain ethnic groups rather than from others. For example, the drinking patterns of Americans of Irish and Scandinavian background and to a lesser degree of native Americans of long ancestry encourage a higher rate of alcoholism than do drinking patterns of Jewish- and Italian-Americans. Reasons for these differences were discussed in detail in Chapter 2.

4

ALCOHOLICS:

vulnerable personalities and drinking groups

Many persons in America—especially younger males—have a "readiness" for alcoholism. Their bent lies mainly in personality makeup,[1] although a high gastric tolerance for alcohol may also contribute. (Someone with low tolerance will be less likely to expose himself to the sharp discomfort that comes to him from even mild drinking.)

The unique ingredient in the process of alcoholism, however, is the fit between vulnerable personality traits and drinking-group values and roles. Thus personality readiness is necessary, but in most instances it is not all-important. Many persons have emotional traits similar to those of alcoholics, but they lack regular exposure to drinking groups that turn latent tendencies into alcoholism.

The person with a readiness for alcoholism finds, in many drinking groups, experiences that deeply gratify his emotional needs. Often these groups reflect subcultural values, such as utilitarian norms for heavy drinking that further cement the personality to an excessive use of alcohol. Also, as has been already noted, drinking groups vary widely in their standards of acceptable drinking behavior. In so doing, they provide an opportunity for finding new emotional support should rewards turn to rejection. Without the encouragement of drinking associates and the chance of replacing drinking-group support from new sources, many persons who lean toward alcoholism would run far less risk.

More specifically, this social-psychological scheme for explaining alcoholism has the following parts: (1) personality features that set the stage, making one a candidate; (2) qualities of drinking-centered groups that uniquely attract and reward the use of alcohol for such persons, linking "readiness" with alcohol; (3) the uneven, but usually inevitable, shift from reward to rejection within drinking groups; and then (4) the seeking out of more tolerant drinking companions, providing continued support and protection for alcoholism to develop.

Vulnerable Personalities: Sociocultural Factors

Individual personality consists of the emotional needs that are relatively unique to a given person plus the adjustment methods he uses to meet them. For example, one may feel a strong need to reduce his anxiety about his sense of inadequacy. To do this he may learn that he feels more comfortable, in American society, if he works very hard and gains recognition for his accomplishments. So he compensates for his concern about himself by overwork. In short, one's personality is formed by a continuing system of numerous motives which act to meet emotional needs made up of the learned tensions and self-sensitivities of daily living.

Both the emotional needs and the ways to fulfill them are products of social learning that an individual experiences in his social milieu. Although the infant years are of critical importance in setting the individual pattern of adjustment techniques to meet emotional needs, later years are also important. Social learning of needs and how to adapt to environmental pressures continues well into mature adulthood.

Cultural values and patterns of social organization play an enormous role in defining these emotional needs and ways to meet them.

Although the values vary in intensity among various segments of society, such as social classes in America, and among discrete individuals in the society, they still influence the socialization of most Americans. In infancy through adulthood, developing personalities learn, first from family and peer groups and later from school and occupational life, certain value complexes. From these value complexes, or concrete themes, come specific needs and adjustment techniques. We shall dwell on those value complexes in American society which contribute directly to various kinds of addictions, especially alcohol.

Arnold Green, in a classic study, has described how middle-class American cultural values may produce a deep sense of dependency in the young child.[2] Parents, who greatly value parental love, can exaggerate this love so that it becomes overprotection, or what Green terms "personality absorption." In return for their sacrifices parents expect the child to love them. As a result the child learns to need love and to meet the anxiety of its possible removal with dependence and obedience.

As the child grows older, however, the value of individual success and achievement and the importance of independence, self-control, and the striving for competitive status enter the socialization process. But because the child has been conditioned to dependence rather than to independence, he is unable to compete as effectively as his parents now urge him to compete. So he begins to doubt his adequacy. He also learns to feel guilty about his dependence and may compensate by outward shows of bold independence.

Basically, American culture, operating through family and peer groups, has taught him, on the one hand, how to be dependent and return love, and, on the other hand, how to be competitive and impersonal and to triumph over others. In an effort to manage both of these sources of emotional needs, he typically fails and comes to feel increasingly inadequate and guilty. He begins to feel ambivalent, tending to depend upon his immediate milieu for guides to his behavior. Yet even as he moves into adolescence he still yearns to be dependent upon the understanding love of his mother. With such a need just in the background, the adult tends to manage it by retreat and withdrawal from competitive relationships when he can conveniently do so. But even in withdrawal he feels angry with himself for giving into his feeling of insecurity and fear of failure in interpersonal situations.

What has been called the "Puritan ethic" in American culture is cause for the child to learn other social values.[3] There is substantial rejection of the developing child's sensual, or organic being, by home, church, and neighborhood. In contrast, his intellectual development receives great emphasis, along with economic success, unselfishness, love, and equality. Having deeply internalized these social values, specific personalities may be particularly attracted to excitement, anger, and immediate gratification of bodily needs such as hunger and sexual pressures.

Finally, developing personalities can be differently exposed to an absence of orienting values or norms which would guide behavior. Those regularly exposed to rapid changes in basic values due to such disorganized influences as frequent migration, family breakup, or occupational mobility, experience an almost unconscious searching for a stable source of moral values. For example, the clash between the ideals of individual freedom and bureaucratic regimentation, between material aspirations and spiritual denial, between the sanctity of the individual and manipulation of persons for personal ends, between some relatively fixed way of life and the rapidity of technical change, if compounded within one experience, can leave a social emptiness that forces the individual to seek some fixed value identity.[4]

One caution, however, should be emphasized. As noted earlier, in no sense do these cultural themes form a common value complex or lack thereof. To imply that they do would be grossly misleading. They impinge on given individuals differently. It is when they converge on one person with the full force of their weight and conflict that a high personality vulnerability for alcoholism or other addictions appears.

Let us turn from the sociocultural factors contributive to a personality vulnerable to alcoholism to examining the personality features of the alcoholic himself.

Personality Traits in Alcoholics

Efforts to study the personality makeup of alcoholics have taken three approaches. First, and most frequent, have been ex post facto studies; i.e., once a person showed clear symptoms of alcoholism his personality pattern was analyzed. Though the logic was questionable, it was then assumed that traits discovered at this point were also present at the onset of the disorder. Second, efforts to study long-sober alcoholics have proceeded on the notion that personality traits are fixed even though they may be stretched by an experience such as alcoholism. Once sober for a substantial period, the original personality returns to its state prior to alcoholism. Finally, there are those tentative efforts to describe personality features present before the onset of the disorder by longitudinal follow-up or by reconstructing the alcoholic's experience.

Regardless of approach and despite many problems of logic and research technique, specific personality traits in the alcoholic repeatedly become apparent from these studies and observation. A combination of these traits makes up the maximum of readiness for alcoholism. *In and of themselves, they do not equal the disorder.* Nothing in the nature of these predisposers inevitably leads to a loss of control over drinking. Also, as we shall see presently, these personality traits appear frequently in many nonalcoholics.

Snyder suggests that one characteristic recurs often—a compulsive independence and therefore an effort to be overly masculine.[5] A potential alcoholic has intense dependency needs and sharp feelings of worthlessness, self-hate, and inadequacy, which produce an unusual need to be looked upon by others and by himself as a "man." To adjust to these feelings, alcoholism-prone persons of either sex try to show no signs of weakness. Observation of dry alcoholics discloses that they frequently challenge authority figures in an effort to cut the authority figure down to size. To cover up the persistent anxiety about their weak self-image, they seek opportunities to show what they can do, even at the expense of their incomes, jobs, and damage to others.

Deep anxiety about one's own adequacy and a thin veneer of

toughness covering it leaves one very susceptible to environmental influences. Thus potential alcoholics easily and rapidly may arrive at a point of view in one particular relationship, only to shift when in a different social context. So their notions about themselves and others lack consistency. The term "passive personality" seems to sum up this kind of behavior that varies markedly with changing situations. Witkins describes these persons as apparently dependent upon the immediate milieu for their responses.[6] This in turn gives rise to acute indecision or ambivalence.

⌊ Because of their anxieties and poor self-esteem, alcoholism-prone persons often withdraw from typical social exchange and adjust by isolation. Many relationships hold the threat of severe damage to a highly sensitive self-image. So it is much easier to maintain a facade of strength and independence by avoiding many interpersonal, competitive relationships.⌉ Such avoidance permits anger to grow from uncorrected notions concerning what others are thinking and doing. Delusions easily multiply and become an almost chronic rage, both toward others and self. Anger toward others develops because of supersuspicion and unfounded threats. Anger increases toward themselves for not having the independence, will power, and manliness to face the situation rather than to withdraw or vacillate.

According to Connor, the natural result of these sentiments is a longing for the warmth and acceptance of primary-type group life.[7] Because adjustment by withdrawal produces social emptiness and a lack of emotional response from others, there is a strong yearning for the comfort and protection of an uncritical, loving set of close intimates among whom accomplishments are readily recognized and uninhibited behavior is absorbed. Since such demands are not typically fulfilled in an impersonal and complex society, persons with such feelings do not easily fit into most social situations. These persons make unrealistic demands on associates and relatives for acceptance and emotional response. They cannot shift perspectives; they lack social skill.

A corollary exists in that these persons exhibit a low threshold of response to excitement, danger, and trouble. The glee of escapades, the thrill of antisocial behavior, the sparkle of aggressive conflict loom large in the subjective narratives of alcoholics about the early period of their malady. A yearning for the new, the different, and the unusual accompanies these histories. Frequently "dry" alcoholics say that they miss the excitement of a good fight or the break in boredom that comes from marital conflict.

[All of these described traits make up an egocentric personality. Button concludes that there is an absence of deep emotional response despite a surface charm and affability.[8] The intense need for a favorable self-image produces a superficial sociability and likableness. Despite the longing for love and acceptance, the desire to be the center of attention cripples the ability to share intimate emotional feelings with others. Also, alcoholism-prone persons tend to seek immediate release from tension. They find it difficult to tolerate frustration and impulsively grope for quick relief from anxiety. In seeking self-centered goals they often disregard accepted rules of honesty and courtesy and become expedient manipulators, readily resorting to falsehoods and deceit.]

Persons made ready for alcoholism by these previously described personality features run even greater risk of becoming alcoholic if they grew up completely unfamiliar with alcohol. Unprepared for what alcohol does to behavior and unacquainted with subtle norms and standards that accompany drinking behavior, they lack learned controls if they should begin to drink. A classic example of this situation was found in the study of Mormon college students mentioned on page 24. Once drinking began, they had a significantly higher number of alcohol-related problems than did student drinkers from backgrounds of drinking experience. Apparently ascetic religious groups keep their members from having sanctioned experience with alcohol. As a result the alcoholism-prone personality among them who begins to drink fails to learn restraint and is more susceptible than ever.

Though these readiness factors of personality and socialization occur often in America, they are not peculiar to alcohol addiction. Many unhappy and neurotic people use alcohol and do not become alcoholic. In spite of the fact that women take up as many mental hospital beds as do males and the relative number of females in out-patient and private psychiatric hospitals is probably greater than that of males, the alcoholism rate for women is much lower than for men. In a study of Italian culture, Lolli found that among Italian-Americans neurotic traits seldom led to uncontrolled use of alcohol.[9] In several studies of psychiatric impairment among both rural and urban nonhospitalized populations, at least 20 percent were found to have serious psychiatric problems and only a small percentage were free of symptoms of psychiatric significance.[10] Yet in contrast, only about 6 percent of the drinkers in America become alcoholics. We must conclude from these facts that clearly another series of factors, more definite than psychological defects, leads to actual alcoholism.

Qualities of Drinking Groups That Reward Ready Personalities

Recall that, in part, drinking persists in America because it enhances sociability within a variety of specific groups, for example, tavern cliques, cocktail parties, ceremonials, and recreation or dancing groups. We shall refer to such groups as "drinking groups." Repeated exposure to these drinking groups tends to satisfy emotional needs of the ready personality, to bring about certain emotional rewards for him, and thereby to fix the use of alcohol as his main adjustment technique.

Hampered by anxiety about his adequacy and harboring persistent anger and delusions, the ready personality learns that alcohol blunts and eases the tension of these psychic pains. Because drinking groups accept the use of this effective tranquilizer, the alcoholism-prone person within the group is relieved of the guilt feelings he might have about openly using an anesthetic that has more than usual value to him.

Drinking groups further satisfy emotional needs by allowing casual participation free from the competitive tone of other interpersonal situations. In a drinking group, the alcoholism-prone person experiences self-confidence and can interact with less fear of damage to his ego and less suspicion of others. Authority figures slip out of role and can be more easily challenged. Chances to express verbal hostility and aggression come more readily, helping to reduce pent-up rage and resentment toward others.

The belief of members of many drinking groups that drinking indicates masculine virility adds to the facade of strength that the ready person badly needs. By proving through drinking that he is a man, he can compensate for his feelings of inadequacy and worthlessness. Several male tavern drinking groups studied by this author drank for purposes of demonstrating virility.[11] Also within these groups "holding your liquor" was a status-giving ability. The group recognition for those who could drink others "under the table" was much higher than for those who passed out or got sick or just went to sleep. The group pressures encouraged continued drinking without appearing intoxicated. The fact that this esteemed high tolerance was a sign of early alcoholism was irrelevant to the status-awarding process. It satisfied emotional needs of the prone person by strengthening his self-image.

Further ego-enhancing opportunities occurred within these same groups through sexual exploits. Long linked with alcohol, sexual conquest offers further proof that one is masculine and strong. Thus within these drinking groups "holding your liquor" and "making out" offered a twin way for feeling truly independent and for enhancing status.

Alcohol is one of the few drugs that can produce a group feeling quickly, and in this fact lies the chief reward of the drinking group. The "we-ness" believed to be basic in primary groups is stimulated by alcohol even in groups whose members may have little in common—witness one cocktail party. With use of alcohol, members of the group tend to communicate more intensively, setting the scene for more cohesion. Acceptance of mild deviation in behavior increases, and rejection is slower than in nondrinking groups. Members of a drinking group are expected to take on a role of outgoing friendliness and of bantering good fellowship. Though the group feeling contrived by alcohol is only temporary, it is particularly gratifying to one inclined toward alcoholism. The longing for primary-group relations is briefly satisfied, and the sense of isolation is temporarily reduced by acceptance and easy emotional response.

Other rewards offered by the drinking group are chances to know different people and to hear about new ideas and experiences as well as to relate some of one's own. The typical role as a drinker calls for one to be charming, to impress others of his worth and to be generally likable, even if he must practice lying and alibiing. Thus the role calls for some measure of attention seeking and ego-centeredness. All of these actions can further shore up a poor self-image.

Since the intimacy of the drinking group is only superficial, the drinker need not become deeply involved emotionally with others. He can have his cake and eat it too. He can secure group-approved release from tension and at the same time avoid repeated, long-term, face-to-face relationships demanding deep emotional involvement, such as takes place in a genuine primary group. Thus many drinking groups might be referred to as pseudoprimary groups.

The fit between personality readiness and qualities of the drinking group forms the basis for learning to turn to alcohol. There is an attraction between personality content and typical drinking-group content. If repeatedly reinforced, drinking becomes the predominant way of coping with the exaggerated emotional needs that make up the readiness. *Alternative ways of adjusting to psychic tension recede and gradually disappear.* Among both males and females some form of group tutelage is a crucial variable in the progression toward alcoholism. It is true that once the drinking group and the ready personality have been linked, the emerging alcoholic, particularly the female, can continue to develop without the group satisfactions, but at the start the ready personality "goes steady" with the group.

It is important to note that groups vary in the extent to which they sanction heavy drinking, and that therefore persons susceptible to alcoholism are differently exposed to regular heavy uses of alcohol. Lower alcoholism rates among women than among men illustrate this difference in exposure. Remember the double standard of inebriety, i.e., that in most drinking situations the drunken female is severely frowned upon though drunkenness is sometimes accepted for males. As a result of this widespread norm, men who drink are more apt to be exposed to heavy-drinking norms, while women run less risk of such exposure.

Among susceptible males there exists a difference in exposure to heavy-drinking norms. A study by Rogers of drinking among fraternity members on a college campus showed that pledges living in fraternity houses conformed to norms calling for much higher use of alcohol than did pledges living in dormitories, while nonfraternity men in dormitories faced the lowest drinking expectations.[12] In another study of young males who were excessive drinkers, Wellman concluded that all belonged to social groups in which regular drinking and drunkenness were accepted and approved.[13]

Studies of first drinking experiences further reveal the correlation between excessive drinkers and exposure to heavy-drinking-group norms. Ullman learned that excessive drinkers tended to experience alcohol initially with friends with whom they drank to a point of intoxication and who ridiculed them for being unable to hold their liquor.[14] Other evidence suggests that an individual's frequency and amount of drinking comes from close friends or spouses rather than from other sources such as the preceding generation.

High alcoholism rates among Irish-Americans probably are partly due to their high exposure to heavy drinking groups. There is no reason to believe that any unusual physical differences reside in being Irish. However, a definite subcultural factor may be involved. A large proportion of Irish-Americans are descended from immigrants from rural Ireland. Descriptions of this particular Irish subculture, especially that presented by Arensberg and Kimball,[15] support the notion that drinking may perform the function of a substitute for sexual relationships in traditional Irish culture. Among the rural Irish, it has been traditional for males to postpone marriage until they have acquired their own farmland, which often occurs quite late in life. Drinking among these unmarried males appears to receive some degree of positive sanction, probably because of the implicit function it serves in reducing frustration anxiety. There is reason to believe that the norm of accepting heavy drinking has been transmitted down through the generations of Irish-Americans without this accompanying function.

In contrast, a study of Jewish male alcoholics, whose histories I recently collected, revealed the potent influence of repeated drinking with heavy-drinking groups. Despite their background of only ritual drinking associated with religious worship, and despite a strong feeling that drunkenness was a gentile vice, these men had become alcoholics. Their drinking habits strongly suggested that they had become assimilated into heavy-using gentile drinking groups. Indexes of personality implied a definite readiness but less than expected.

In sum, heavy-drinking groups with norms that define alcohol as having extraordinary personal effects for the individual member contribute sharply to alcoholism. Such evidence raises the possibility that repeated participation in such heavy-drinking groups may bring on alcoholism without the prerequisite of unusual fears or anxieties. According to Hanfman, merely by complying with the norms of steady, heavy drinking a group member may become an excessive drinker.[16] In a sense he is processed into chronic alcoholism. In a larger sense the entire group collectively moves toward uncontrollable drinking, the members supporting each other in the process. In extreme cases, such as the "lush" groups of skid row, and in less extreme instances, such as tavern drinking groups, members underparticipate in conventional social life but are fully socialized within their tight-knit drinking groups. Most drinking groups, however, lack such cohesion and tolerance.

Rewards Become Rejection

Despite the possibility of emotional reward, drinking groups are also sources of social rejection. But negative sanctions that define and penalize undesirable drinking behavior are weak, irregular, and infrequent, contrasting clearly with the abundance of rewarding positive sanctions. Therefore, though ostracism does occur as the alcoholic progresses into his illness, it builds up very slowly and fitfully.

I have observed various drinking groups that revealed this slow development of disapproval and suggested that the group acceptance received by the excessive drinker seemed to increase his resistance to any group pressure. In other words, the more the excessive drinker was accepted, the less worried he was about conforming, and the more he felt free to deviate.

These observations further suggest that, for a time, the deviant seems to have real value for the drinking group. In some instances heavy drinkers, who clearly drank much more than others, were taken home in order to prevent accidents, were briefly hidden to avoid police questioning, and were provided with sufficient money to keep on drinking. In one group it was possible for an excessive drinker to drink for entire weekends at practically no expense to himself.

Dentler has concluded from a study of nondrinking groups in army barracks, where schizophrenic deviants received a peculiar kind of acceptance and became the objects of paternal "protection," that groups offer numerous alternatives short of rejection and that deviants function to help the group to define its own boundaries of what is acceptable behavior.[17] In drinking groups this function is the same, and, in its process, the developing alcoholic continues to get attention, acceptance, and encouragement for his behavior. By using alternatives short of rejection, the drinking group provides a protective umbrella under which the uncontrolled drinker can develop.

Though acceptance and rejection of deviation vary, and though deviation is briefly rewarded, a point can be reached, nevertheless, where the excessive drinker is completely ostracized. Into the rejection is incorporated the almost ubiquitous social value of *self-control*, which lies in the deepest levels of American consciousness. This crucial social value of self-control sets the stage for social rejection of the alcoholic and for the social isolation and sense of guilt which characterize the alcoholic in our culture. Without this crucial social value of self-control there would probably be far less chronic alcoholism in the United States. It is indeed ironic that the very values that produce the most admired behavior in our society also aid in the etiology of one of our most severe public health problems.

Because he, too, feels his lack of self-control, the excessive drinker himself gives impetus to the process of exclusion. Long practiced in withdrawal techniques to adjust, he himself begins to reject his drinking associates. He is apt to resent them for rejecting him and because they can control their drinking and he cannot. Thus his sense of social apartness grows.

The group acceptance and emotional rewards experienced earlier fade, and resentments and self-hate take their place. The drinker finds two ways of managing his renewed psychic pains: alcohol and an accepting group milieu. Increased drinking reduces significantly the subjective feelings of loneliness, resentment, and self-hate and sets the stage for seeking out others with whom he can drink heavily without being unusual. Unable to accept himself as "normal" and facing signs of exclusion, he voluntarily withdraws from original drinking friends and situations and seeks new ones where he can reexperience the same satisfactions and reduce the same psychic pains. This time, however, these pains are greater, requiring more alcohol, and the drinking groups must be more tolerant in order to provide him greater freedom from the negative sanctions experienced earlier.

New Drinking Groups: Excessive Drinkers Become Segregated

Finding new and rewarding drinking companions is, however, a groping process. The drinker enters upon a period of "shopping around," of exploratory and tentative approaches to persons who seem to have the same problem of adjustment that he has.[18] This is apt to take the form of a half-unconscious "feeling out" of new situations; he wants to find out how new or different drinkers accept and satisfy him. Even these quests are usually done in the company of another disaffected person with whom some emotional ties have already been made. His groping is interactional rather than private.

Furthermore, in scouting around for a chance to reestablish himself in a new social scene, the alcoholic is very sensitive to loss of self-esteem and emotional support from others. He tries to avoid losing whatever status feelings he now possesses. In so doing he is apt to look among lower-status possibilities where his drinking companions will continue "to look up to him."

On the other hand, downward social movement is only one possibility. In an urban, complex community there are many chances to find and participate in easygoing, heavy-drinking groups in the same broad social class. The important point is that the drinker seeks new groupings which tend to reward the drinking behavior that was socially rejected earlier. Since this is an effort to affiliate with new drinking groups, it may or may not be a matter of geographical traveling. Such social shifts can readily occur in the same town or city.

Here is a short description by a fifty-year-old accountant of his feelings during this middle period of his drinking problem:

The reason why I went to the lower places was because the other guys, although I wouldn't admit it, were beginning to look down on me. The better class, the class I had slipped away from because I became miserable and mean when drinking, were beginning to say I couldn't manage the stuff. Because I had to step over the deep end, I looked for the other guy who had stepped over the deep end too. Because I wanted to make myself really believe I really wasn't so bad I tried to find such drinkers. I always had to feel superior. If someone looks down on you, and you can't cope with it, you're going to go somewhere where you can cope with it.

Opportunities to "relocate" vary socially. Group solutions to the adjustment problem may be next to impossible. Female alcoholics again provide an example. They feel far less free to seek out new drinking companions and in trying have fewer chances of finding female drinkers to accompany them. They are more likely to "go it alone" without a network of emotional and even economic supports made up of drinkers with similar problems. On the other hand, the incipient female alcoholic who disregards these pressures probably has more opportunity than her male counterpart.

In general, however, chances to establish ties with more alienated drinking groups are good in our society. In some instances the process is capricious and moves without effort. But mostly it is a matter of deliberate experiment.

At this point the marked ambivalence about alcohol among Americans plays a crucial role. Since we lack uniform folkways and traditions to govern drinking norms, informal drinking groups mirror a wide variety of tolerance. One can move without undue effort, however, to a more permissive group. Unlike other deviations, such as organized crime, homosexuality, or drug use, induction into deviant drinking groups can be more rapid, requiring less group tutelage and making the drinker feel less of an "outsider." The upshot is simple. An early-stage alcoholic who feels the strain of initial deviation can, without too much effort, find others who are experiencing similar strain and also seeking group support.

In essence, the ready personality has moved another step toward his alcoholism. He has replaced the drinking companions who "cold-shouldered" him with ones who drink as he does and with whom he can reestablish most of the psychic rewards he knew before. The price he pays is not very much. The rewards make up handily for the weak and confused social punishments and threats. He has probably met with few clearly defined, forewarned, automatic negative sanctions and so has little reason to fear anyway.

Tavern drinking groups are examples. Different taverns set their own norms of what they will tolerate. Developing alcoholics can shift from the less tolerant to the more tolerant without too much effort. They may increase their participation in the more tolerant without completely giving up their part in the less tolerant. So the alcoholic probably becomes well known in many different taverns by "making the rounds." As a particular drinking episode progresses he may move steadily toward the taverns with more indulgent group norms. Or he may make a sharp break and tend to concentrate on one, moving on to another if the rejection process sets in.

Notice here the sharp contrast with Cantonese Chinese drinking groups in New York City's Chinatown and with Jewish-American drinking groups, especially those close to Orthodoxy. Among these two ethnic groups no opportunity, short of complete severance of community ties, is available for shifting to more lenient drinking groups. The social stigma of excessive drinking plays inexorably upon the deviant, leaving him little chance to escape. So he conforms rather than risk loss of all emotional support with little chance of support elsewhere.

Where social controls break down because of a weakening of community ties, chances for alcoholism go up markedly. The Jewish alcoholics discussed earlier all showed a definite loosening of social ties with the Jewish community. In most instances a complete break had removed the social barriers of the community, which in turn had led to the alcoholics' affiliation with deviant drinking groups.

Finally, a process of progressive isolation can set in. The reward-rejection-relocation experience recurs, leaving the abnormal drinker even further excluded and with even more tolerant fellow drinkers. This shifting from intolerant groups to more tolerant ones provides a network of group supports. The more group shifting of this kind takes place, the more isolated from typical drinking patterns the alcoholic becomes. He may migrate into drinking groups where will power plays practically no role at all in defining acceptable behavior.

In facing the many problems of middle-stage alcoholism—supply, severe hangovers, protection during binge—the alcoholic finds both economic and emotional support from fellow tipplers within his heavy-drinking cliques. The symptoms of alcoholism—the "shakes," for example—continue to provide the prestige, the recognition, that "holding your liquor" had given earlier. And, since many of its members have the same symptoms, there is an atmosphere of acceptance, of uncritical jocularity, of "That's nothing, I've had those lots of times."

Exclusion Becomes Permanent

Up to this point, the excessive drinking behavior of the alcoholic has come from the fit between his personality readiness and the character of drinking groups. Now, however, a third factor—unalterable social segregation—becomes clearly operative.[19] It acts to "lock in" alcoholism securely as a behavior pattern. As the alcoholic drinks and associates with other heavy drinkers, general community disapproval sets in. In upper strata of society this social reaction, though more limited, is nonetheless operating. In middle and lower-middle strata the excessive drinker is more visible, and the isolating forces are potent. At the lower extremes of the social classes he may receive little general exclusion. In sum, however, he and those with whom he drinks usually become widely identified as deviants. Various pockets of rejection have combined into a permanent stigma.

Some type of formal labeling may cap off this process. The alcoholic may be arrested several times for public intoxication or drunken driving. His wife may publicly separate or sue for divorce. He may seek out "drying-out" places or be diagnosed an alcoholic in a public hospital. These labels step up the isolating responses of those in his life space. He and those who drink as he does reach a point of no return. They have segregated themselves, and the community has reinforced the isolation. There are practically no social paths on which they can reenter normal, conventional society. Undefined deviation has become organized into specific deviant roles within stigmatized groups. Practically speaking, these roles call for excessive, abnormal drinking. Anyone in such a role is expected to act like a "drunk" and usually does so. A self-image as an alcoholic, different from other drinkers, is a direct result. Accordingly alcoholics seem to identify easily with one another; almost subconsciously they seem readily to know one another. Their apartness from others is almost complete.

As the process moves along, those personality features that made for readiness in the first place become even more exaggerated. Well-defined by others as deviant, the alcoholic's self-hate is now thoroughly validated. Repeated experiences with exclusion feed his already well-formed delusions. His resentments and fears of others become organized and even further removed from reality. Even if he had a rather low "readiness" to begin with, a series of rejection-exclusion experiences could precipitate personality patterns of this type.

On the other hand, the exclusion experience continues to produce, even to increase, emotional satisfaction. Antisocial tendencies are now expected behavior. The possibility of excitement, danger, and trouble goes up. Being excluded justifies aggression against those who were the excluders. The lack of a "way back" to normal acceptance frees the alcoholic to seek the very new and different. Escapades of various kinds are consistent with the self-reaction engendered by his role as a pariah.

Also rewarding is the close "in-groupness" he can experience intermittently with other stigmatized, excessive drinkers. Among them he can counteract the tormenting hopelessness of loss of control. Because they arise from sharing similar exclusion experiences, the emotional bonds are even stronger, the primary-group emotions more genuine. The alcoholic can interact with a group of similarly stigmatized persons who aid him to cope not only with alcoholism but with all the by-products of estrangement from acceptable society. In emotionally charged, interpersonal relations of this kind his deep feelings of anomie, of social apartness, find some relief.

Thus the emotional traits in "readiness" and the symptoms of alcoholism expand with the exclusion process. Just the opposite happens to the alcoholic's opportunity for treatment. The isolation process shields him from confronting a clear definition of his drinking problem. It also prevents him from confronting consistent negative sanctions and punishments. Support in a new group delays a sense of "hitting bottom." For example, with such support the alcoholic tends to hesitate to affiliate with Alcoholics Anonymous.[20]

We can summarize, therefore, by stating that in American society—especially middle-class America—a process of social isolation from the larger society rather than one of social control within it completes the alcoholism progression. The process begins with the fit between vulnerable personality traits and drinking group qualities and proceeds with rejection by one set of drinking groups and reaffiliation with a more tolerant one. When heavy-drinking groups themselves become unalterably segregated from "normal" drinkers, the organized reaction of the general community converts limited rejection into full-scale social isolation. When this occurs, the alcoholic continues to drink but is socially walled off from the central institutions of American society.

One unique dominant social value—self-control—validates this entire process. Persistent loss of control of the emotions and of actions, because of drinking, violates this pervasive moral value, justifying exclusion. Because of social ambivalence and confusion about alcohol, Americans activate this potent moral value slowly; but once under way, it is a major impetus in the segregation of those addicted to alcohol.

This explanation of alcoholism is relatively peculiar to America. Because sociocultural forces are different, for example, in France, among the Camba, or in Italy, the theory cannot be applied there. Apparently sociocultural factors peculiar to America produce vulnerable personalities and segregating forces which isolate heavy-drinking behavior. Some day a theory of drinking pathologies may be applicable to many types of societies. In our present state of knowledge, however, we must be content with a limited effort, which when generalized to cultural units other than the United States will not suffice.

CHAPTER 5

IMPACT ON FAMILY AND WORK LIFE

Alcoholism and Marriage

That alcoholics accumulate in the mature ages and develop in all social strata makes for a sharp impact on one of our central institutions, the family. Contrary to popular notions, large segments of the alcoholic population are either married or remarried. The often-arrested police-court inebriate tends to be "never married," and the homeless alcoholic of skid row has participated even less in marriage; but large numbers of alcoholics come from middle-class groups, have rarely encountered the police, have been married but often divorced, and are in a regular job. As spouses and as employees, they have found their illness to have a disrupting influence on marital relations, on children, on bosses, and on fellow workers.

Statistically speaking, middle- and upper-class alcoholics marry at about the same rate as the general population, but they show a higher number of broken marriages than comparable, nonalcoholic groups. This applies to both male and female inebriates. Despite this high rate of separation and divorce, however, the majority of alcoholics continue to live with a spouse. Apparently a drinking problem poses no serious barrier for a divorced alcoholic seeking to remarry.

When the police-court inebriate and homeless types of alcoholics are combined with the more stable patients often seen in voluntary clinics, the entire alcoholic group shows significant marital differences from age-comparable nonalcoholics. Studies by both Jackson and Bailey have shown that the alcoholic is more often single, divorced, separated, or widowed.[1] In essence, abnormal drinkers experience less on-going marital continuity than do nonalcoholics.

Because alcoholics marry as often as they do, the lives of many nonalcoholics are affected. Wives, husbands, parents, and children must adjust to the presence of a problem drinker. Since the American family, made up chiefly of the sexual unit and offspring, is an organization, each member has to have a predictable role. Unless the roles are regularly fulfilled by all members, the smooth functioning of the family breaks down, resulting in confusion, uncertainty, and a clouding of roles. According to Jackson, at least two to three other family members are affected adversely by an alcoholic relative.[2] Under these conditions, at least twelve million persons, including the abnormal drinkers themselves, suffer from the impact of alcoholism on the family.

Most is known about the impact on wives and least about how children are influenced. Earlier studies of the family concluded that certain types of women tended to select alcoholics or early-stage problem drinkers as husbands to meet unconscious "mothering" needs. Such wives, it was maintained, have an unconscious need to maintain, absorb, and "suffer" their husbands' active alcoholism. This notion, however, has since proved to be dubious as a single explanation. Some subtle personality factors probably do influence the wife to encourage her husband's alcoholism, but the improved adjustment of many wives following their husbands' sustained sobriety throws doubt on the hypothesis.

Much more indicative of alcoholism's impact on the wife is her reaction to the progress of her husband's disease. Often the end result of living through such an experience is deep personality disturbance, but it is doubtful that the wife was deeply upset at the beginning of her husband's drinking problems. More probably her groping efforts to cope with the puzzle of her husband's behavior produced severe problems of adjustment. The following analysis relies heavily on the work of Jackson and Lemert.[3]

Impact during Early Phases

Although drinking has often been a problem for a man before marriage occurs, his new wife may not have recognized his proclivity during courtship or for some time after the wedding. Developing alcoholics are often charming people, and many men who are not alcoholics drink to excess on social occasions. Soon, however, the wife begins to notice embarrassing incidents, usually in a social situation. Her husband's behavior exceeds what other drinkers expect of him. He may badly stagger or become overaggressive. More likely, he will become hilariously overactive, insisting on directing the band or demonstrating his wrestling prowess or becoming overly amorous with other females present.

At first the wife may overlook these deviant actions, but as they recur, she begins to worry about the opinion of other people. Discussions with her husband, however, and his periods of controlled drinking or no drinking at all tend to reassure her. Then the inappropriate drinking events, followed by urgings from the wife and periods of controlled drinking, are repeated in rapid succession. However, because of the identification in the public mind of alcoholism with late-stage skid-row-type drinking, the wife, like so many others, may not understand what is happening. She often feels she is somewhere at fault and seeks to change. Discussion of deviant drinking episodes becomes strained, and soon both try to forgive and regain the idealized image of romantic love.

As the uncontrolled drinking occasions multiply, however, the wife begins to define her husband's behavior as a clear problem and a threat to the family's reputation. Efforts to discuss the problem meet with mixed hostility and repeated promises. His reasons, alibis, and excuses confuse her for a time, but soon the sense of threat to her and her marriage reappears. So she tries to help him control his drinking. She may agree to drink with him, both of them stopping at a certain point. She may buy the liquor in an effort to control the amount available at home. She may search out liquor he could have hidden and secretly dump or water it.

As a part of this control effort, she engages in cover-up and a determined campaign to understand why her husband drinks as he does. Sharing with him the cultural compulsion to manage their own problems without outside help, she redoubles her efforts to camouflage and eliminate the abnormal drinking. She may recruit the family doctor to provide legitimate "sick" diagnoses for her husband's "unbearable" employer, who "causes him to drink too much now and then." Children's queries receive vague and indefinite answers.

As her attempts to contain the problem repeatedly fail, so does her rapport with her husband deteriorate. Less and less does he fill the role of father and husband, and more and more she must take over both male and female family roles. No longer can he be depended upon to arrive home on any reasonable schedule. Whether or not he will use his paycheck for legitimate family expenses or "spree" a large part of it away is unpredictable. Often the wife learns of garnishments, levies, and other salary or wage assessments at work to pay debts she did not know existed.

Her bewilderment increases when out of his guilt and self-hate, he tries to recapture the romantic charm of his courtship and early marriage days. For a brief time she becomes "queen for a day," and quickly her belief in his eventual self-control reasserts itself. Again she thinks of the alcoholic as a skid-row bum or a police-court "drunk," unemployed, homeless, in trouble with the law, and because her husband is not like that she abandons her ideas of doing something about the problem.

But her respite is usually short-lived because of sudden shifts in her husband's behavior. Once fun-loving, charming, and affectionate when sober, he changes to a demanding, touchy, abusive, even cruel person when drinking. If ordinarily reserved and shy, he becomes boisterous, maudlin, overly sentimental and reckless, especially in spending money. After such personality changes, the wife's hopes soar high only to be repeatedly dashed by his inability to control his drinking.

Throughout this early period the family remains intact. Wife and children make gestures of deference and obedience when the husband is sober. When he is drinking the wife tries to maintain a front which implies that her husband's role is merely temporarily suspended. This pretense indicates her continuing effort to deny and eliminate the problem and the absence of any socially patterned way to manage it. Friends are kind and often counsel patience. Such key persons as family doctor, lawyer, and minister are often as baffled as she is, and there is always the undying hope that he will "get hold of himself." In devising ways of getting on with family living, the wife begins to derive her emotional support and satisfaction from her children, not her alcoholic spouse.

The Middle and Late Symptoms and Marital Life

As the wife is struggling to maintain the formal family pattern, outside forces move the family into a middle period of adjustment. Friends include them less and less in drinking-group situations, and both the wife and her drinking husband withdraw more and participate less in outside social activities in an effort to cover up and avoid further humiliation. The exclusion from friendship groups serves to verify the wife's fears about her husband's drinking.

As these anxieties and fears crystallize, a cluster of new reactions manifests itself. The wife becomes resigned to the inability of herself or her husband to control his drinking and decides that further effort is useless. Overt hostility, anger, and resentment are expressed by both, and the wife may refuse sexual relations with her husband. She may then begin to doubt her ability as a wife and mother and to hate herself for her outbursts and futile attempts to confront the problem. For example, if she seeks and finds her husband at the moment he gets paid, she may appear foolish in her attempt to secure his check for family needs.

Conflicts over the children tend to be pervasive during this period. The wife's concern for them and the deep split with her husband often lead to a search for outside help. For a middle-class wife, this is the acme of psychic pain. It is an admission of her helplessness and her husband's alcoholism. Any present personality disturbance is precipitated into crippling fear· and anxiety because of the unpredictability of her husband and of the hard blows to her self-respect.

By means of outside help and through her own sense of despair, she completely replaces her husband. The two openly compete for the loyalties of the children, but because of his growing sense of rejection at home and his growing acceptance among other alcoholics, he finally withdraws, leaving the field to her. She replaces her husband as manager of the house, financial controller, and disciplinarian. Because of her own guilt feelings, she may continue to pay his bills, provide his bail, lie to his employer, praise him to the children, and nurse him during a drying-out period, but for all practical purposes he is husband in name only.

When the wife partly stabilizes the family without her husband, she reestablishes some faith in herself and provides a basis for rethinking the situation. Perhaps reading about alcoholism or talking with doctors, ministers, local agencies, or members of Alcoholics Anonymous will lead her to discover that treatment facilities do exist for her alcoholic husband. She may learn that she need not cover up or be ashamed, at which point she may decide to remain married. If so, she must continue to manage the family during her husband's therapy.

Should the therapy be successful, the wife will have to relinquish her role as head of the family, permitting her husband's reentry and altering the family pattern back to its original one. Still there is the latent fear of relapse with its threat to security and social acceptance and the probable need for children to have to adjust again to a new series of authority roles.

From·the marital statistics it is clear that often the wife decides to terminate the marriage. She has discovered that while managing on her own, her family runs more smoothly and she has more security. She believes her children have a more consistent and less confusing environment.

In sum, it seems doubtful that wives are deeply upset at the beginning of their husband's drinking problem. On the other hand, the demands to adjust to new family roles created by living with an alcoholic spouse could result in personality disturbance. Although far less is known about husbands of alcoholic women, it seems probable that living through the experience leaves him just as disorganized.

Impact on Children

Much the same can be said about children of alcoholics—especially if the alcoholic is their mother. Although this impact has been greatly exaggerated, it seems reasonable to believe that children are adversely affected. If they are infants or quite young, or if they are well into adolescence, the damage to them may be less; but in preadolescence they suffer a variety of emotional handicaps. The sudden changes in parental personality deprive the child of the security of predictable behavior from an intimate authority figure. The unpredictable behavior of an alcoholic mother—alternately loving and rejecting the child—may lead to feelings of rejection and isolation. Experiences with an alcoholic father may be less intense but inconsistent enough to confuse. A child may anticipate certain rewards only to be frustrated. In seeking some measure of control over his environment he fails.

An alcoholic parent also deprives children of adult role models. Obviously an alcoholic father provides an inadequate male model. The mother, trying to perform two roles in such a situation, often does well in neither. If the marriage terminates, one role is not present at all. If the alcoholic father successfully seeks treatment, he upsets the family role patterns when he reenters the group. Children also experience the social ostracism of the family, the intensity of which varies; it can be damaging to a child's self-image and can sharply limit normal interpersonal experiences.

[There is also some evidence that an alcoholic parent exposes a child to a higher risk of alcoholism. Bleuler found that the incidence of alcoholism among children of fifty high-status alcoholics was higher than in the general population.[4] Roe, in another study, discovered that the high expectancy of alcoholism among children with two alcoholic parents did not happen when they were studied after growing up in foster homes.[5] Another series of data suggests higher rates of anxiety and depression neuroses among alcoholics' children when matched with those of nonalcoholics.[6]]

Alcoholism in Industry

Since, contrary to popular belief, the bulk of alcoholics are in the early and middle stages and have both homes and jobs, they have an impact on the work world as well as on the family. For example, job performance suffers in numerous ways: supervisors, fellow workers, and union officials must deal with a series of baffling behaviors; executive alcoholics cost their companies thousands of dollars in poor decisions.[7]

The alcoholic is usually employed during most of his illness. Thus, in the early and middle stages and even when approaching the chronic late stage he typically continues to work. Alcoholics appear to be evenly distributed among various occupations and industries.[8] All levels of management and the professions have their share. Recall, however, that the alcoholic is concentrated in those sex and age categories that aggravate his impact as a personnel problem; thus he is lodged in the productive ages of thirty-five to fifty and is predominantly male—traditionally the breadwinner. Despite speculations about there being as many female as male alcoholics, no evidence has as yet disproved the maleness of the problem —especially in the work world. For practical purposes we can use the figure of 3 percent to estimate the probable number in any particular organization. This figure varies up or down with specific conditions such as sex ratio (the more women in the company, the fewer the alcoholics), or age distribution (the younger the work force, the fewer the alcoholics), but it is still a good modal figure.

Specific Job Behaviors

Impaired work performance is the major impact of alcoholism on the job. Prior to and during the early phases, the alcoholic is at least an average employee, and often he is a superior one. As his illness progresses, however, his job efficiency declines. Members of Alcoholics Anonymous describe a substantial decrease in work effectiveness during the middle stage of their alcoholism.[9] Tiring out quickly, increased frequency of mistakes, and an uneven frenzied work pace mark this decline. Supervisors of alcoholic employees, who rated them with other employees during the middle to middle-late stages of alcoholism, consistently saw them as closer to their worst employees than to their best.[10] Comparing their work performance with that of other emotionally disturbed workers (such as neurotic and psychotic ones), bosses rated alcoholic employees as performing the poorest. These low estimates held despite occupational status. They centered around poorer and less work results, the need for an inordinate amount of supervision, and various forms of absenteeism.

Absenteeism aggravates poor work performance. Maxwell reports that male alcoholics have almost three times the sick absences of a matched control group.[11] I found alcoholic employees in one large company to have five times as many ten-or-more days of absences as did a representative group of employees.[12] On the other hand, neurotic and psychotic employees also had excessive stay-away absences, but alcoholics were more chronic; i.e., their incidence of absences and actual number of days absent began and continued over a longer period of time.

Alcoholics also showed other forms of absences in addition to the traditional off-the-job type. Unlike other absent employees, they often failed to report their absences. Also, once at work they would disappear from their work place—"partial absenteeism." In addition, they engaged in what AA members call "on-the-job" absenteeism. Thus an employee will physically, but not mentally, be on the job. This is especially true with professional, managerial, and other white-collar personnel, who tend to go to work even when feeling unable to do an effective job.

In contrast to absenteeism, an unusual number of on-the-job accidents does not characterize the middle- or late-stage alcoholic. In the very early period of his drinking he seems to be more accident-prone than other employees,[13] but as his problem becomes worse, he has fewer job-related injuries. One reason for this is his high rate of absenteeism. Exposure to accidents is greater among lower-status alcoholics where off-the-job absenteeism is high. Apparently these drinkers feel they are particularly apt to have an accident on a particular day and therefore do not go to work. Instead they tend to have off-the-job accidents of a rather minor type.

Another reason for few accidents lies in the alcoholic's efforts to deny there is anything wrong with him. He becomes extra cautious at work, realizing that an accident would probably spotlight him and his drinking problem. In addition, fellow workers and immediate supervisors, who typically know about his drinking problem, often act to reduce his exposure. For example, if he seems to them to be feeling particularly bad, they may maneuver him to a safer but temporary spot.

Alcoholic employees show about the same job turnover pattern as nonalcoholic employees.[14] The notion that they are job hoppers comes from the skid-row stereotype. I have concluded that turnover experiences reported by a group of AA members reflected turnover patterns of the labor force in general rather than job changes characteristic of alcoholism. Thus among these subjects job mobility was relatively low in occupations for which extensive training or experience is required and substantially higher among operatives and laborers. If anything, the same subjects suggested a tendency to stay on a job, once hired, since almost 40 percent reported no changes at all over the seven to ten years of the early and middle stages of their drinking problems.

Additional support for this trend comes from a study of alcoholic employees in a large Eastern utility company. Whereas the non-alcoholics were spread evenly over various tenure categories, the alcoholics were concentrated significantly in a group with twenty-one to thirty years of service. In practical terms these points mean that many alcoholics develop their illness while on only one or two jobs. It also implies that an employer can expect his alcoholic employee to remain with him rather than losing him either voluntarily or by discharge.

One final job-behavior pattern should be discussed—cover-up of alcoholism symptoms. Here again, the common notions about supervisors energetically covering up their alcoholic employees seems to be more myth than fact. Thus 40 percent of a group of AA respondents said they themselves did the most to hide their drinking problems while on the job, while approximately 20 percent had no cover-up experiences at all. Of the remaining 40 percent, 19 percent said fellow workers were the most effective cover-up agents, 12 percent so described their immediate bosses, and 9 percent said subordinates did the most to cover up.[15]

These cover-up experiences varied by job status. High-status managerial and professional subjects tended to describe a form of self-cover-up, implying a sizable amount of freedom from close supervision plus a desire to present a "normal" appearance when drinking with work associates off the job. In contrast, low-status respondents reported themselves performing few, if any, cover-up efforts. They seemed uninhibited about their problem, drinking openly with work associates off the job. They depended upon work associates to cover for them.

Reaction of Immediate Supervisor to Alcoholic Employee

We have seen the experiences the wife is apt to have with an alcoholic husband, but to broaden our focus we also need to ask the question: What happens to his immediate supervisor at work?

The boss typically interacts specifically and closely with subordinates in an emotionally charged relationship that makes him a "significant other" for his employees. He is in a position to define impairment of work performance and apply negative sanctions if performance is poor.

How, specifically, does he react? In answering this question I shall rely on my recent research findings.[16] First, supervisors of an alcoholic employee were generally aware of his drinking problem as he moved toward the middle stages. Certain behaviors and signs indicated to the boss the presence of developing alcoholism. Seen fairly early and frequently, thereafter, were such clues as leaving his post temporarily, other forms of absenteeism, unusual excuses for absences, lower quantity and quality of work, red or bleary eyes, and hangover symptoms. Although the typical boss did not realize that severe alcoholism might well be an end result, he, as well as fellow workers, did connect these behaviors with deviant drinking. In short, despite the alcoholic's efforts to cover up, he was anything but hidden from the boss.

Second, in this study, all supervisors of alcoholics classified them as definite supervisory problems, in sharp contrast to bosses of diagnosed neurotics, who often saw these employees as superior workers. Thus alcoholics were supervisory headaches because their bosses had to spend much more time supervising them than other employees; they were unpredictable, so that the boss never knew what to expect; their various kinds of absences forced the supervisor to make last-minute adjustments; and, because their work effectiveness declined, they had a bad effect on fellow workers who felt they often had to do the alcoholics' work for them.

Despite the fact that supervisors of alcoholics consistently designated alcoholic employees as problem employees, they were more indecisive about taking corrective action than were bosses of either problem neurotics or psychotics. Like the wife when her alcoholic husband treated her royally for a short period and was a model husband, they were impressed by those periods when the problem drinker would "snap out of it" and do an ultragood job for a short period of time. If the alcoholic had been with a particular supervisor before his drinking problem developed, he was usually recalled as having once been an able employee and well liked by fellow workers. If the boss had come up through the ranks with him, he had another reason to hesitate.

When the supervisor considered referring the alcoholic employee to the treatment facilities of the company medical department, even more potent barriers entered his thinking. The biggest one was his belief that he should keep the problem within his small domain and somehow manage it himself. Like the alcoholic's wife, his boss believed he could contain and resolve the problem. In short, it was his duty as a line supervisor, not that of the medical department, to handle the problem. Other blocking attitudes reinforced this do-it-myself feeling; he might not be supported in such a move by his boss; the union might challenge his action; referral might mean discharge or separation; and there is a sentiment among the alcoholic's fellow workers that such matters should be "kept among the boys" and not referred to staff people like the medical and personnel departments. Behind these barriers lay the pervasive skid-row image, which the boss also shared with the wife; and since the alcoholic was not like this image, the boss hesitated to take any action.

These forces pushing and blocking the supervisor put him on what one man called a "seesaw." Rather than making a willful and deliberate cover-up of his alcoholic employee, the boss was pushed both toward taking action, on the one hand, and putting up with the alcoholic, on the other. In many ways it was easier to do the latter than directly to confront the employee with a simple, straightforward account of his behavior. To confront the problem-drinking employee was to confront his own guilt, ambivalence, and anxieties about drinking. It was more comfortable to avoid facing the realities. Furthermore, the unpleasantness of not knowing what to say or how to say it, the pressures of many other ongoing, specific, immediate problems, and the general reluctance to invade the employee's privacy were always present.

Company Programs and Policies

Because of the problem presented by the alcoholic employee, some United States companies have devised specific personnel policies and programs aimed at rehabilitation.[17] Usually the policy stems from one main point: Alcoholism impairs both the quantity and quality of work; consequently the company can legitimately enter the employee's life. With poor work as a basis, most policies set forth three main guidelines: (1) Alcoholism is a health condition, not a moral defect; (2) as with other illnesses, the company will help the alcoholic employee to get treatment; but (3) unless reasonable recovery takes place, based on professional prognosis, the company, in conjunction with the union, will discharge the employee. As we shall see in Chapter 7, this policy of "constructive coercion" aims at producing a crisis in the employee's life. This crisis, in turn, reduces the possibility of an alcoholic's denial of a drinking problem and makes him more amenable to therapy.

The organization with this policy faces specific problems of implementation. First the company assumes that poor job performance can be pinpointed and used as a basis for confronting the employee, but performance appraisals are often too superficial to serve this purpose. In addition, realistic treatment facilities must be available because, unless they are, there is little reason for supporting the employee with, for example, sick leave. Some companies rely on their own medical departments, while others use community resources. Probably the main problem, however, is in the attitude of line-operating supervisors. Unless they use the policy, it becomes mere words, and, as we have pointed out, there are numerous reasons for them to resist its use. As a result a gap develops between policy and practice. Top management and staff people, such as industrial physicians and personnel managers, may support and urge the use of the policy, but actually it is at the mercy of the operating boss.

On the other hand, we also noted in our study that the supervisor has positive reasons to follow the program; hence the problem is to reduce his reluctance and stimulate those forces pressing him to take action. Two ways may be used to do this: (1) supervisory training and (2) use of informed, neutral staff people. If training is geared to the problem employee in general, not to the alcoholic employee in particular, supervisors show less resistance and more favorable reaction to new information about alcoholism and a company's policy. A traditional frontal approach invokes all the defenses already described. In addition, a nonthreatening staff person with some special knowledge, such as an industrial nurse, can aid in bridging the gap between policy and action. She occupies a role and possesses enough expertise to help the line boss as he tries to make a decision. At the same time she is not viewed as an authority figure as would be a higher manager, personnel director, or industrial physician.

Unions and Alcoholism

Competing with this gap between policy and supervisory action as a barrier to effective use of an alcoholism policy is the attitude of the union toward the policy. Much like the wife and boss, union officials such as shop stewards and business agents vacillate about taking any action: On the one hand, these union officials display deep concern about the alcoholic and his family. They believe, in theory, that it is a good thing to support the company's efforts in the interests of employee welfare. On the other hand, to do so looks to many union members like collusion with management, especially if the man is discharged. In addition, they share with the supervisor the same unwillingness to confront the alcoholic—and the fear that backing referral to the medical department will result in discharge.

Private arbitrators, employed to resolve grievance disputes between union and management over discharged or disciplined alcoholic employees have provided, in their decisions, guidelines that help to reduce the union's ambivalence. Of the forty-six reported arbitration cases over the past ten years involving alcoholic employees, arbitrators have reinstated half of them. This is a significantly higher reinstatement rate than is found in the typical discharge case. The principal reason given by arbitrators for reinstatement revolves around the company's obligation to provide meaningful treatment and rehabilitation opportunities. As a result, several companies have turned to joint union-management rehabilitation efforts. If union officials realize that arbitration decision trends about alcoholic employees tend to underscore the responsibility of management to supply treatment support, they will be able to reduce their indecision.

Role of Work World in Reducing Alcoholism

There are numerous reasons why company-based personnel policies and programs on alcoholism offer the main opportunity for making realistic progress against alcoholism.[18] For many an alcoholic a secure job situation is his most convincing proof, both to himself and to his critics, that he still controls his drinking. It is his last bastion of defense. When his work suffers and his supervisor confronts him realistically about it, as he would do under a "constructive-coercion" policy, he faces, probably for the first time, a situation he cannot manipulate. The reality of his actual behavior is clearly revealed to him. The matter is out in the open, accompanied by an opportunity for treatment.

Furthermore, since developing alcoholics in the early and middle stages of their disorder continue to work, they are regularly in an ongoing situation where they are visible to bosses, fellow workers, and union people. Thus the relatively early- and middle-stage symptoms can be seen and identified on the job. True, the earliest signs are skillfully covered up by many alcoholic employees, but, as the middle symptoms begin to appear, they are readily visible in the work environment.

A final reason why the work world can contribute heavily to the treatment of alcoholics is that it can bring to bear the influence of two potent institutions—management and unions—at the same time. If both of these can confront the problem drinker in a collective, rehabilitative fashion, a combined force operates that is available nowhere else in American society. Of course home and church in combination can often exert an influence, but it is without the impersonal authority of management combined with union. The union member tends to see his union as a means of protection on the job. The alcoholic who is a union member thinks of manipulating this protection to his advantage. If the union tells him, in effect, the same thing as the company, he is more likely to rethink his situation and accept the treatment offered him.

Job Factors That Contribute to Alcoholism

Certain features of jobs and organizations aggravate the vulnerability of alcoholism-prone employees. Demands for rapid adjustments to either sharp job content or organizational changes are examples. Foltman concluded that the prospect of being retrained for an unknown job presented a near traumatic problem for high seniority, unskilled, and semiskilled factory workers.[19] Mann and Williams found that white-collar office workers who had been at the center of intense changeovers to electronic data-processing equipment showed more psychological and physical anxiety than similar white-collar groups in the nation.[20] When such changes accompany organizational changes, such as a rapid shift in upper-level management people, the complex of events presents some personalities with high risks to their mental health. In short, it heightens their susceptibility to alcoholism. If automation and other types of drastic job-content changes can be introduced in ways that anticipate the human reaction and permit successful adjustment, these risks will be substantially reduced.

Because of the amazing pace of technological change, it is probable that many highly technical, professional jobs will soon have spans of only one to fifteen years.[21] This job-obsolescence experience can be most damaging to an already weak self-image. I have collected case histories of alcoholic electrical engineers which suggest that the approach of "job old age" precipitates heavier drinking in a personality already attracted to a pathological use of alcohol. Furthermore, some jobs often make temperamental demands which do not fit the personality of the jobholder. A personnel manager, for example, is required to enter into all kinds and types of interactions with fellow employees. In a given day he may interact with union officers, top management, lower-level supervisors, run-of-the-mill employees, his own staff, other staff people, to say nothing of community functionaries like United Fund representatives. In sharp contrast, a night watchman works in social isolation. His job requires him to adjust to an absence of other people and to the self-reliance generated by their absence. Obviously a mismatch of personality and job demands produces frustrations and a sense of inadequacy and failure. Employment offices in industry have the responsibility of reducing this emotional health risk by closer matching of job and personality, thereby reducing the likelihood of mismatched personalities turning to alcohol.

Finally organizations often informally stimulate the belief that drinking is an important part of performing a job. Thus work histories of sales managers,[22] purchasing agents, and international representatives of labor unions who have become alcoholics strongly suggest that their organizations tacitly approve and expect them to use alcohol to accomplish their purposes effectively. Some organizations have decided to include in their personnel policies a point about the role alcohol is expected to play in various jobs that might involve its use, pointing out that such jobs can be performed effectively without alcohol. On the other hand, the policy usually states merely that the company does not believe alcohol is necessary and gives the employee full right to decide.

6

OPIATE ADDICTION:

a comparison with alcoholism

Since getting a perspective on alcohol and alcoholism in America is the major aim of this book, a contrast of alcoholism with dependence on opiates would further broaden our view. We shall focus on opiates and opiatelike drugs since they make up the major source of drug addiction.

The "Dope-fiend" Image

Opiates—principally opium, morphine, and heroin (the latter is the strongest of the three)—have not always had the odious image that attaches to them today. In the United States, if we examine the period prior to the Civil War, we find that patent medicines of all kinds containing some opiate derivatives were sold without any controls and that physicians used forms of opiates to treat many symptoms of illness. As a result, addiction to opiates did occur, but it was not so labeled, and a good deal of sympathy was shown addicts who often continued to function fairly well.

The Civil War itself focused additional attention on opiates and their use when morphine by injection was used to reduce the pain of thousands of wounded soldiers. These wounded veterans became easily addicted and remained so for life. Many secured their own hypodermic needle equipment, and it was this needle that came to symbolize a growing concern and a changing attitude about opiate addiction. To give oneself an injection was somehow undesirable. Still, as Isbell relates in a study of the development of attitudes toward opiate addiction in the United States, even at this time few addicted veterans were harshly stigmatized.[1]

The dope-fiend stigma that exists in the United States came from two sources: race prejudice and confusion of opiates with cocaine. As a powder, opiates look much like cocaine, but the effects of the two drugs are quite different. Opiates are depressant drugs; cocaine is a stimulant. Repeated use of the latter causes peculiar behavior, including possible delusions of persecution, gross trembling, and mental confusions. Users are truly "jazzed-up," and are apt to assault or harm others. To equate the two drugs would be quite natural, attributing to the use of both the opiates and cocaine very disagreeable behavior.

Probably the most potent source of the dope-fiend stigma, however, was racial prejudice. Opiate use became associated with foreign groups and strange behavior. To Chinese laborers, brought to the West Coast in large numbers just after the Civil War, smoking opium was a part of everyday living. It was a folkway much as beer drinking was among German immigrants and wine drinking with meals was among the Italians. According to Isbell, as long as these Chinese provided the hard labor for building the railroads west, they and their opium-smoking custom were accepted and even popular with those seeking new experiences.[2] But when the Orientals became a menace to jobs and competitors in business, prejudice began. During this time, criminal elements began to adopt and exploit the opium customs of the Chinese. Further imports of laborers from China aggravated these conditions, causing a fear of a "yellow tide," and in 1888 Federal legislation cut off all Chinese entry.

Still opiates continued to be associated with foreigners and with crime. Addicts often came from Jewish or Italian backgrounds and exhibited delinquent behavior. Since World War II opiate addicts have come largely from Negro and Puerto Rican ghettos in urban areas, reinforcing the notion that certain racial groups engage in the loathsome practice. Recently Mexican migrants to large cities have contributed a disproportionate number of addicts.

That these immigrant addicts did not bring the practice with them is shown by low rates of addiction in areas from which they migrated. Their relation to crime comes from their being concentrated in areas with highest delinquency rates, often showing a significantly higher nonviolent crime rate. It also comes from the fact that the fantastic prices currently paid for opiates force most addicts into crime. Moreover, the addict must use the moneys from his crime to purchase opiates, which are themselves illicit goods. He is thus a "two-way" criminal, associated with a very profitable and well-organized pattern of crime.

The Harrison Act and Later Antinarcotic Laws

Unlike the prohibition of alcohol, the prohibition of opiates has been widely accepted in the United States. Federal law has been severely interpreted and administered, but unfortunately such administration has proved to be ineffective. Prior to 1909 some states had laws forbidding the smoking of opium, but Federal tariffs impeded these laws by legalizing its import. As the tariffs were raised, smuggling of smoking opium was increased; this was the beginning of the illicit market.[3]

Further control by the Federal government had its beginnings in international events. The Spanish-American War brought to the attention of various people in the government the presence of opium smoking in the Philippine Islands. Investigations by the United States interested the Chinese and later the British. In 1909 the Federal government made treaties with China prohibiting all opium trade and requested the help of the British in convening a worldwide conference on the trade of opiates. At this time concern was further heightened when it became obvious that heroin, first isolated from opium in 1898 and thought to be nonaddictive, was actually as addictive as opium or morphine, if not more so. The conference, which occurred in 1909, was followed by a second in 1912 called the Hague International Opium Convention. The result was a loose agreement, in which most of the countries of the world agreed to limit growth of and trade in opium to amounts needed for medical and scientific use only. Each signer pledged its government to enact laws limiting the use of opiates exclusively for medical and scientific purposes.

To carry out this pledge in the United States, the Harrison Narcotic Act was passed in 1914, but its execution did not really get under way until after World War I and coincided with efforts to execute the Volstead Act on the manufacture and sale of alcohol. Based on Federal tax power, the Harrison Act required that the import, distribution, and sale of opiates be a matter of record subject to investigation. It set up a system of licensing to control the persons who could distribute the drugs and to whom they could be sold. Licensed physicians could prescribe or administer opiates legitimately as a part of professional practice.

The Harrison Act was administered, however, with unintended and distorted results. As many addicts to opiates discovered their sources drying up, they sought out unscrupulous physicians who prescribed narcotics for profit and not for genuine therapy. A tiny minority of the medical profession exploited the law to the point of antagonizing fellow professionals and enforcement officials. Physicians engaged in such practices were arrested and, in a series of Supreme Court cases, were judged to be engaged in nonprofessional practices. Some of the language of the court implied that physicians, regardless of their intent, should not prescribe opiates for one addicted to the use of the drug. Therefore, as Lindesmith has described, most doctors become wary of treating an addict for fear of Federal prosecution.[4]

The physicians' fear intensified following the interpretation of the Harrison Act in the Behrman case of 1922. At this time the refusal of many doctors to treat addicts had caused the concentration of patients in public facilities. Public clinics were established which soon came to dispense large amounts of drugs to addicts for self-administration. The medical profession clamored for the removal of these clinics and for the prohibiting of all ambulatory treatment. In the Behrman case, the Attorney General sought and got a Supreme Court ruling that supplying drugs to addicts for self-administration was improper professional practice.

In 1925 the Court partly reversed itself and ruled that a physician acting in good faith could give moderate amounts of opiates to an addict to relieve the distress of withdrawal. The Court concluded that earlier cases had involved flagrant abuse and, furthermore, that the Harrison Act was a revenue and licensing act saying nothing about addiction. However, in spite of this reversal, the Behrman case has remained the basis from which stems the Federal execution of the Harrison Act. Physicians still remain afraid to treat addicts because Federal agents can accuse and arrest them, and a jury must decide the extent of their "good faith."

On the other hand, efforts actually to suppress the sale and use of opiates have been largely unsuccessful. Both state and additional Federal laws, despite their severity, have failed to reduce materially the amount of addiction. A Federal statute, the Boggs Act of 1952, imposed a mandatory sentence for narcotics offenses.[5] The Narcotic Control Act, passed by Congress in 1956, raised the minimum sentences for offenders and permitted the death penalty for those who sell narcotics to persons under eighteen years of age. A patchwork of state antinarcotics laws emerged during this period,[6] but despite these punishments, addicts notoriously relapsed and "got back on."

Unlike physicians, who were frightened by the harsh administration of the Harrison Act, addicts and suppliers were encouraged to become criminals. Cut off from a legal source of drugs, the addict readily sought illegal sources rather than face the horror of withdrawal symptoms and the frustrations of a life without drugs. The well-organized sellers found in the laws an opportunity for fantastic profit at relatively low risk of being caught—especially those who controlled the market. Clinard estimates that on an investment of approximately $6,000 a crime syndicate can realize from $40,000 to $60,000 profit.[7] With such prospects the smuggling and selling of opiates becomes a well-organized, profitable business despite law-enforcement efforts.

Definition of Opiate Addiction

The World Health Organization defines drug addiction as a "state of periodic or chronic intoxication produced by the repeated consumption of a drug. Its characteristics include: (1) an overpowering desire or need (compulsion) to continue taking the drug and to obtain it by any means; (2) a tendency to increase the dose; (3) a psychic (psychological) and generally a physical dependence on the effects of the drug; (4) a detrimental effect on the individual and society."[8]

Basically, an opiate addict is a person who feels normal on drugs. He is physically and psychologically dependent on the presence of an opiate for a sense of well-being. Physical dependency centers around the addict's *tolerance* for the drug. Tolerance refers to the increase in amounts of the drug a user must take in order to maintain the same effects. As the user increases his amount, his body adapts to the presence of the drug in such a way that he can take dosages that would be deadly to a nonuser. Psychological dependency centers in release from the frustration of daily living with its competitive demands. The association of opiates with a "cool world" produces for the addict a craving that seems to be independent of tolerance. Even though he may have been off drugs for months or even years, this emotional attachment remains, and it goes on regardless of his physical condition. So an addict can be defined as one who is not only "hooked" physically through unusually heightened tolerance but is also hooked emotionally.

The crippling effect of the addict's physical and psychological dependence on opiates is evidenced in the severe withdrawal symptoms (hangover) which occur when he is first without the drug. At this time he experiences days of living hell, at first becoming nervous and restless, then having chills and fever accompanied by vomiting, diarrhea, and stomach cramps. In addition, he experiences muscular pains, especially in the torso, often accompanied by the "shakes," running nose and eyes, and insomnia. All these agonies combine to create excruciating mental and physical tortures, relief from which is obtained only when use of the drug is resumed. Otherwise the distress will slowly subside over a period of four or five days to a week. Although the symptoms of withdrawal distress vary in severity from addict to addict, they are rarely less intense than a bad and prolonged case of flu. In order to obtain costly, illegal drugs to prevent these severe withdrawal symptoms, the typical opiate addict must repeatedly steal enough to buy drugs from an ultracriminal subculture, the narcotics racket. Here he is quite unlike the alcoholic, who can usually obtain his supply easily and legally.

Prevalence and Distribution of Opiate Addicts as Compared with Alcoholics

Also, unlike the millions of alcoholics, opiate addicts are estimated in only the thousands. In 1960 official estimates of the Federal Bureau of Narcotics listed 45,391 active drug addicts in the United States. These are, of course, only the known users. Every labeled case probably represents at least two unidentified cases. For example, a New York City study estimated there were ninety thousand addicts in that city alone.[9] Even so, the numbers are small when compared with those of alcoholics.

Whereas approximately seventy million Americans used alcohol, only between three and five million become addicted. This is less than 10 percent. In contrast, according to expert opinion, most regular users of opiates become dependent on them.[10] Hence the incidence of addiction among steady users of morphine ·runs about 70 percent; among users of heroin it is almost 100 percent. So to speak of a regular opiate user is, typically, to refer to an opiate addict.

Another difference between alcoholics and opiate addicts can be observed in age concentrations. Since it usually takes years of drinking to become an alcoholic, the greatest number are found in the mature ages, while opiate users are clearly concentrated in youthful categories.[11] A majority of the arrests for Federal narcotics violations during 1955 were under thirty years of age. Out of 1,844 new drug-addict cases found in New York City from 1949 to 1952, a majority became addicted in late adolescence.[12] The Illinois Institute for Juvenile Research reported that of the estimated 7,500 opiate addicts in Chicago in 1952, over 60 percent were between seventeen and twenty-five.[13] On the other hand, both kinds of addicts are predominantly males.

In clear contrast to alcoholics, users of opiates are sharply concentrated among specific ethnic, racial, and social class elements. Only 25 percent of all narcotic addicts reported by the Bureau of Narcotics in 1961 were of white origin. Negro, Puerto Rican, and Mexican immigrants to our large urban centers contribute the large majority. Because they cluster in certain parts of large cities—New York, Chicago, Philadelphia, Baltimore, Detroit, and Los Angeles—opiate addicts are usually a part of a deviant subculture among the most deprived of America's population. They congregate in transition neighborhoods at the bottommost levels of society, which are characterized by poor housing, high rates of juvenile delinquency, poverty, disorganized family life, and stigmatized minority groups. Here they easily associate with other addicts, readily contact peddlers, and are less visible. In New York, for example, close to 90 percent of the cases fall in only 13 percent of the census tracts.[14] In some of these tracts as many as 10 percent of the males between the ages of sixteen and twenty years were drug users during a three-year period.

One group of opiate addicts does not represent the typical group described above. Oddly enough, numerous physicians—who represent an extremely high occupational status—are also addicted to opiates.[15] Both their knowledge of what opiates do and their access to legal sources apparently make them especially vulnerable. Since, however, there are relatively few doctors, and estimates indicate that only one in every 100 is addicted to opiates, physicians contribute only a small fraction of the total number of addicts.

If we further examine the characteristics of drug addicts in this country, we find that their numbers are disproportionately high among those who commit nonviolent property crime and crimes for profit (robbery, larceny, unlawful entry).[16] They are unusually low among those who commit offenses against persons—assault, rape, and disorderly conduct. Clearly, addicts commit crimes chiefly for immediate financial gain, because of the great cost of the needed drugs. They do *not* engage in personal crimes, because the immediate effect of opiates actually dissolves antisocial hostilities. Here again they contrast with alcoholics, who show some association with crimes against individuals rather than property.[17] Since alcohol releases learned inhibitions, this relationship seems due to the direct results of alcohol on behavior. The relationship, however, is less pronounced than that between drug addicts and property crimes.

Additional Differences between Opiate and Alcohol Dependency

Americans look upon the use of heroin or morphine—both derived from opium—as the ultimate in depravity. The existence of severe though ineffective laws prohibiting the use of opiates and of special units to enforce these laws indicates the intensity of feeling among the general public. Taking advantage of this feeling, temperance groups often equate the use of alcohol and the use of opiates in an effort to identify the alcohol user with the stereotype of the dope fiend.

The fact is, however, that obvious differences between the alcohol user and the opiate user do exist. Some people think the user of alcohol is immoral; most think he engages in acceptable behavior. The opiate user, on the other hand, is seen by almost everyone as an utterly degraded person. Furthermore, unlike alcohol, opiates reach users in a highly illegal and clandestine fashion.

A marked difference can be observed in the intoxication of the opiate addict and that of the alcoholic. The opiate addict's performance is hurt most when he is without the drug, whereas the alcoholic's performance suffers most when he begins—and necessarily continues—to drink. The difference lies in the effects of the two drugs on behavior. Alcohol releases inhibitions, permitting gregarious and unpredictable behavior and preventing consistent, effective performance. Opiates, in contrast, act to weaken aggressive drives, including sex drives, and permit the addict to go about his daily routine appearing and feeling normal. The effects are quieting and soothing. The user experiences a sense of euphoria and freedom from emotional needs and anxieties—a general sense of detached well-being. Once "hooked," he finds the tremendous anxiety about withdrawal distress dissolved by the effects of the drug.

The process of becoming addicted to opiates also differs sharply from becoming an alcoholic. In opiate users a rapid and high tolerance for the drug usually occurs, while tolerance for alcohol accumulates over a period of years and rarely exceeds the initial tolerance by more than three or four times. According to Jellinek,[18] opiate users often take amounts five to six times greater than the typical lethal dose within weeks after the initial experience. Because of this rapid development of tolerance to opiates, the initial effects also decline quickly, calling for a higher intake or for a period of nonuse in order to regain the full effect upon starting again. Even though both the opiate addict and the alcoholic have little control over their need to continue using the drug, the opiate addict never had much control to begin with. The alcoholic can often think back to times of social controlled drinking.

Because of the rapidity of addiction to the drug, it is misleading to speak of "early," "middle," and "late" stages of opiate addiction. It is more accurate to talk about how or when a user becomes aware of what the drug does to him. To become an addict, a person must consciously use the drug; that is, he must learn how to administer it and to identify its effects. Lindesmith describes two forces which bring about such an awareness: (1) the intensity of withdrawal distress, and (2) intimate association with other addicts from whom the potential addict learns what the withdrawal distress means.[19] Because even an inexperienced user can undergo the distress of abstinence, it is quite possible to experience the physical pains without connecting them with opiates. For example, hospitalized patients may receive heavy doses and have corresponding abstinent distress without knowing why. If, however, the user has close contact with those who understand the linkage between opiates and withdrawal symptoms, he easily learns why he is physically sick and what he has to do to get relief. In short, he comes to think of himself as someone who has to have opiates to perform normally. When this self-concept appears and is acted upon, the user clearly becomes "hooked." In contrast, withdrawal distress in early-stage alcoholics is much less intense, and they readily understand the linkage between their discomfort and the use of alcohol.

One other difference between being addicted to alcohol and being dependent on opiates should be mentioned. Alcoholism may result in such organic diseases as cirrhosis of the liver or tuberculosis; sexual impotence is the most debilitating disorder related to chronic opiate use.

Social Climate and Personality

Let us further examine the addiction process by studying inherent conditions in our society that lend themselves to opiate addiction for certain personalities, plus the role of social groupings in this respect. Opiate addicts, as we have seen, spring mostly from adolescent groups in the severely deprived sections of large urban centers. The social values of self-control and achievement which motivate many alcoholics have failed to penetrate the small, highly segregated pocket of society known to the opiate addict. Instead, these extremely deprived neighborhoods generate different social values— pleasures of the moment, revolt against conventional society, adherence to street-corner society—and they create a sense of hopelessness and despair in persons facing forces over which they are utterly powerless.[20] Consequently these neighborhoods set the stage for the use of drugs as a source of excitement and a temporary surcease from the emptiness of life.

Furthermore, this lowest level of lower-class strata from which the addict comes provides a background for small, cohesive cliques of addicted users. The mistrust of "them" and the close cohesiveness of "us" favor informal cliques with strong bonds. Family disorganization loosens institutional controls, further encouraging these cliques. A sense of futility and the defiance of convention foster a general tolerance of deviance. For users a bleak, pessimistic outlook on life temporarily melts in the soothing balm of opiates. Finally, this stratum exposes inhabitants to drug use because crime syndicates specializing in the sale of narcotics center their activities here. This differential, ready access to a scarce drug, is probably as potent a causal factor as the disorganization of social life. The physician addicts described earlier support this conclusion. Paradoxically, they were similar to lowest-class persons in that they were exposed to a steadily available supply. Unlike the low-class person, however, the supply for them was legally accessible.

Rejection of the opiate addict by typical user groups does not parallel that of alcoholism. Rejection and segregation of the alcoholic come slowly and fitfully. Isolated deviant drinking groups are few compared with the multitude of acceptable and conventional drinking groups. The rejection process of the opiate addict, however, is much shorter, more clear-cut, and less value-charged. As soon as the addict is "on the stuff," isolation from his gang or street associates tends to take place.[21] Moreover, the legal status of the drug user intensifies the isolation. Not only is the addict of little value to his street-corner gang, but he adds the liability of closer police scrutiny. Thus the rejection of the addict is twofold, in that he comes from a thoroughly segregated population segment to begin with. It is akin to rejection of the alcoholic only when the latter moves into the late stages of his illness.

Although these forces in the social milieu are potent as factors in addiction, they contribute even further by fostering addiction-prone personality types.[22] Impoverished neighborhoods, where the rate of drug addiction is relatively high, are more likely to produce young people with immature personalities fearful of adulthood and of responsibility. In short, personalities with greater vulnerability and susceptibility to drug addiction seem more likely to develop in these areas. A sizable number of young personalities in slum areas are exposed to the use of opiates and use them experimentally for a brief time, but only a portion of these actually become addicted. Personality factors seem to be the selective mechanism that brings them to addiction.

These personality features appear to be more pathological and more disturbing than in alcoholics. Opiate addicts suffer a serious pathology in their abnormal use of withdrawal and isolation as a way to manage the anxiety of extremely low self-regard. In many ways this disturbance arises from the family disorganization so prevalent in neighborhoods rating high in opiate addiction. The presence of some form of unstable condition between parents—divorce, separation, violence and hatred, transitory fathers—tends to deprive the male child of a father figure.[23] Without this role-model he is confused about how to behave and tends to withdraw rather than to relate normally to others. This lack of the male parent also deprives the child of chances to learn discipline and consistent conformity to a degree of rule and authority. It increases the likelihood that the mother may respond on one occasion with overprotectiveness, overloving, and overleniency and in other instances with strictness, hostility, and rejection.

The compulsive independence detected in the alcoholic tends to appear as a deep-seated disturbance in sex identity in the opiate addict. An extreme sensitivity about being masculine intermingles with a passive mother attachment that blocks heterosexual relations.[24] The longing for primary group life is also expressed in this exaggerated mother fixation. The poor self-esteem of the person ready for alcoholism is apparently even more pronounced among drug addicts. The research data clearly suggest that addicts are very dependent, passive persons whose anxiety about fulfilling a masculine self-image is pathological.[25]

In yet other ways the personality features of addicts appear to be enlarged versions of the emotional life of many alcoholics. Very low frustration tolerance and limited social skills appear often as basic themes in the addict's personality makeup.[26] To gratify immediate impulse is a strong need that intertwines readily with subcultural values of "pleasures of the moment." Segregated cliques of addicts demand little of members except a central interest in drugs. They engage in practically no group activities such as ball games, parties, or dances. They share only one simple interest, getting and using drugs. Thus the exaggerated egocentric focus on themselves does not demand intimate emotional sharing. On the other hand, they do get a degree of involvement from such cliques, permitting them a small measure of group identification.

In sum, we can say that the opiate user, with his high anxiety about maturity, masculinity, and group relationships, is probably more ready for the addictive use of opiates than the potential alcoholic is for alcohol. The drugs, themselves, plus the addict's membership in a deviant subgroup, are means of adjusting to a life of hopelessness.

THERAPIES
AND THEIR SUCCESS

There are two basic ways to approach the social problems of alcoholism and opiate addiction: (1) by some kind of treatment after the disorder crystallizes and (2) by prevention efforts aimed at reducing the various ingredients that produce the disorders. Since most current energy goes into treatment rather than prevention, we ·shall look at treatment first. In the final chapter we shall examine various aspects of prevention that should be thought about and acted upon in the future.

Treatment methods can also be divided into two broad types: (1) individual-bound efforts, and (2) efforts that use the interaction patterns surrounding the alcoholic as a therapeutic tool, i.e., group therapy of some type. A combination of these broad types makes up a third possibility.

Within the first or individual-bound type are numerous subtypes: individual psychotherapy, drugs, aversion treatments, and vitamin therapy. The second type, group therapies, include both nonprofessional groups, such as Alcoholics Anonymous and "halfway" houses, and professionally guided groups such as group psychotherapy. In between are "therapeutic communities," psychodrama, and discussion groups of alcoholics with a minimum of professional guidance.

Individual-bound Therapies

Individual psychotherapy refers to classical psychoanalysis or to a modified version of it. In the former the psychiatrist develops rapport with his patient by means of dispassionate listening and questions designed to reveal the alcoholic's unconscious feelings. Often, according to Knight, such an approach assumes that alcoholism is but a symptom of a severe neurosis which must be treated first.[1] The basic aim is to help the alcoholic gain self-insight through a process of reeducation in which he "grows up" emotionally. Treatment is typically lengthy, lasting from eighteen months to two years in analysis. Frequently the focus is upon their reliving the difficult childhood experiences that may have prevented emotional maturity.

Sharing some of the concepts of psychoanalysis is a kind of psychiatry that attempts to accelerate the process of "surrender," i.e., admitting that one is powerless over alcohol. Tiebout has discussed this psychiatric interviewing, which is aimed at patiently seeing the alcoholic through his excuses and denials.[2] Slowly, it is believed, the drinker will come to realize that he must surrender his own efforts to control the situation to the direction of the therapist. The approach assumes that the alcoholic goes through specific therapeutic stages. First he flatly refuses any sort of treatment except as a way to "dry out" temporarily. As his illness progresses, he listens but ignores most of the doctor's suggestions. They are too risky for him. Finally, he arrives at a stage of complete surrender.

Throughout this painful procedure, the therapist allows the alcoholic to progress at his own speed. If the therapist is authoritative he arouses hostility and slows the process. Also, alcoholics have a tendency never to give up, especially when faced with a threat from an expert. Circumstances and time, however, will slowly weaken the resistance. If the therapist has shown patience and understanding, he can exercise substantial influence when the alcoholic approaches the surrender phase.

Various drugs have been used as supplements to psychotherapy. One drug is chlordiazepoxide (Librium), which, according to various studies and reports, seems to be a valuable adjunct both in treating the acute phases of severe, prolonged intoxication and in aiding long-time psychotherapy.[3] For the acute patient, reliable clinic reports show its calming effect on the disturbed and shaking alcoholic when he is experiencing withdrawal distress. Used in conjunction with long-term psychotherapy, this drug fosters a willingness to face reality and admit the true nature of a drinking problem. Moreover, since patients seem less apt to become addicted to Librium, alcoholics do not come to substitute it for liquor as they often do other drugs, such as barbiturates, some other tranquilizers, and pep pills.

Recently, hallucinogenic drugs such as LSD-25 (d-lysergic acid diethylamide) have been used experimentally in treatment. It is difficult to determine whether this drug is an adjunct to psychotherapy, or vice versa, since the profound temporary perception changes brought about by its injection seem to be a central part of some therapy. The drug temporarily alters brain function, creating a profusion of emotional and perceptual experiences which can vary from blissful ecstasy to extreme anxiety. In the latter case the experience may be so terrible that the patient will never want to go through it again, and even a permanently damaged emotional life may result. Unfortunately, LSD attracted a great deal of support before careful and repeated follow-up studies have shown its dangers as well as its benefits.

In any event the main purpose of the drug in treating alcoholics is to produce a single, overwhelming psychological experience, making the alcoholic more amenable to change. The setting in which the experience takes place is crucial in making the experience positive and free from anxiety and tension for the patient. Therapists make elaborate preparations, including advance explanations of possible reactions. Therapists themselves go through the eight- to ten-hour visual experience too.

Older than this type of drug therapy are therapies that attempt to produce, in the alcoholic, an aversion to alcohol. Two that have been in use for years are conditioned-reflex therapy (first suggested as a general strategy by the noted Russian physiologist, Pavlov) and the drug, Antabuse, which is a chemical guard against drinking again.

In conditioned-reflex therapy, also regarded as an adjunct to psychotherapy, the sight, taste, and odor of alcohol and a drinking setting, such as a typical bar, are associated with a very uncomfortable experience—usually uncontrollable retching. Both Voegtlin and Miller have described treatment by this method.[4] The process attempts to set up an uncomfortable response, such as a short-lived illness, to the presence of alcohol.

In conditioning sessions the patient is first exposed to a maximum of stimuli associated with drinking. Then a nauseant is administered to produce immediate and violent vomiting. Just prior to the onset of the dry heaves (often the subjects do not eat the night before) each patient drinks about 4 ounces of whisky of his choice, slowly and 1 ounce at a time. If the timing is good, the smell, taste, and environmental conditions of a drinking situation will coincide with the extreme discomfort of repeated retchings. Usually the alcoholic is given about eight to ten sessions of approximately thirty to forty-five minutes each. Because individuals vary widely, some persons are conditioned quickly; others do not condition after a dozen sessions. Most, however, leave the experience with a feeling of nausea clearly associated with alcohol. As one patient told the writer, "I couldn't see the beer truck drive down the street without getting the dry heaves."

Whether or not the conditioning is permanent is questionable. Some therapy programs arrange for retreatment a few months after the first session. These repeated treatments reinforce the conditioning so that the aversion is more likely to remain.

The other way to produce an aversion to alcohol, by administration of the drug Antabuse (tetraethylthiuram), has been described by Winship.[5] Since Antabuse and alcohol do not mix, a person taking Antabuse regularly knows that if he takes a drink of alcohol he will become violently ill. He will experience recurrent severe flushing of the face and eyeballs, dull pressure headaches, elevated pulse rate, heart palpitations, and difficulty in breathing. Since these effects are still produced for five to seven days after use of Antabuse has been discontinued, the alcoholic must decide in advance whether he wants to drink and avoid the uncomfortable results. Thus Antabuse is a "chemical fence" around the alcoholic, forcing him to be abstinent and supplying time for other therapies to work. For example, Antabuse has in many cases provided the sobriety necessary for a genuine exposure to Alcoholics Anonymous. It relieves the alcoholic of the need repeatedly to decide every day not to drink. He need only take the drug.

It is more than possible that drugs similar to Antabuse may set a limit upon how much an alcoholic can "slip" back into drinking. In a study of alcoholism in Japan, Moore describes a cyanamide compound that allows a patient to drink about 8 ounces of wine per day before an unpleasant reaction sets in. If the patient is unwilling to take the drug, it is put in his food without his knowledge. If he drinks very much, he gets sick. After a few experiences, he concludes that his illness results from excessive drinking and moderates his intake.[6]

Group Therapy

Among the numerous kinds of group therapy used in treating alcoholics, the voluntary fellowship of Alcoholics Anonymous occupies a prominent position. Lacking any professional standing, it has appealed to alcoholics to join with others of their kind in mutual support against the uncontrollable need to drink. In short, it is an unguided, self-help, alcoholic-treat-alcoholic movement, in which alcoholics themselves assume responsibility for arresting their disorder. AA grew spontaneously, without guidance from professionals such as psychiatrists, psychologists, or sociologists.[7]

At both open meetings to which the public is invited and the closed meetings for alcoholics only, AA members frankly narrate their drinking histories and explain how the program enabled them to gain sobriety. Members travel in small groups to adjacent towns to tell their stories and to share their program for sobriety at AA meetings there. Often two or three members will hold meetings in prisons or hospitals where they explain the AA program to alcoholic inmates.

The fellowship of AA, however, is more than this. Local groups sponsor dances, parties, and picnics. Families of the members often form family auxiliaries, such as "Al-Anon" and "Al-Ateen," for spouses and children. Individual members often go together to eat lunch or drink coffee; they meet after work to bowl, to fish, to play cards. These informal contacts extend the fellowship beyond the more formal meetings. In this network of interpersonal relationships, the fellowship's "Twelve Steps" to sobriety make up the core of the effort to remain sober. For example, the first step strikes at the constant denial of a drinking problem: "We admitted we were powerless over alcohol—that our lives had become unmanageable."

Membership in AA depends solely upon whether or not an alcoholic says he is a member. Current members carry their personal histories to other alcoholics and "sponsor" them as novices. This is called "Twelfth Step" work. According to the fellowship's definition, an AA group exists whenever two drunks join together to practice the AA program for sobriety. There are no officers, no hierarchy, no dues.

Although AA is not organized in the usual sense, a common body of tradition underlies the movement. The "Twelve Traditions" set forth the policies that have been effective guides for the fellowship in the past. One of them is a statement of AA's single, explicit purpose: to help alcoholics remain sober. Another is to refrain from embracing any cause, religious, political, or social, except the one of helping alcoholics.

Thus AA is a group endeavor on the part of alcoholics themselves to find a solution to their crippling problem. Out of their face-to-face associations with one another a network of group controls for sobriety emerges that is not present in the usual doctor-patient relationship. Members frequently refer to their experience in AA as a "way of life," since for them it is an emotionally satisfying alternative to chronic drinking. Why does AA work for those alcoholics who do affiliate? Prominent among the reasons is AA's effect on self-concepts. Thus through "Twelfth Step" work the AA member continues to see himself as he used to be. At the same time membership promotes an abstaining, acceptable image of the self. In addition, his role permits him to recapture a respectable social position in the community: AA is truly a "way back."

Another important reason why AA works, once affiliation takes place, is that it sets up a network of social controls, for example, an "in-group" atmosphere that serves as a potent sobriety guide. Furthermore, the primary group flavor of AA, a *gemeinschaft* in a secular, anomic society, gives a member an opportunity to satisfy his need for warmth, reassurance, and dependency.

"Halfway houses," sometimes called "recovery houses," resemble AA to a degree in that they are voluntary, that often members of AA make up the paid staff, that AA meetings are a regular part of the therapy offered, and that AA principles pervade discussions and interpersonal relationships. These halfway houses are relatively small boarding houses set up for low-price, short-range (usually one to three months) feeding and housing for persons who voluntarily admit they have a drinking problem. They may be privately operated, or government-supported to some extent. Even though AA tradition does not permit a direct sponsorship of these houses, many of them act as a sort of extension of AA.

At the same time, the halfway houses go beyond AA notions by enforcing group controls that AA does not have. Rules requiring sobriety are quite clear and quickly enforced by the house manager. The house insists that residents get a job and pay a modest rent. The alcoholic is frequently helped in job hunting. Other forms of counseling are available as a supplement to AA, and "guests" of the house are expected to participate.

Since the network of social controls is ever present day by day, these houses offer a clear potential for therapy. The residents become, for a short time, a part of a social group made up of fellow alcoholics who are partly insulated from the outside world. Here segregated group pressures operate to enforce sobriety rather than to encourage inebriety. From a practical standpoint the house provides a base from which an alcoholic—especially one going into the late stages—can begin a "comeback." Usually he has no way to get a start if he is discharged from a hospital, jail, or clinic. The halfway house aims at providing the minimum necessary to reestablish the alcoholic in organized, respectable society.

Because they have a paid staff, the halfway houses move away from a purely nonprofessional kind of therapy; but rarely are these staff people highly professional. They do, however, frequently conduct discussion meetings in which residents participate. In these meetings the staff person uses discussion-leadership methods to get members involved and talking. In this fashion he hopes to educate about alcohol and alcoholism, on the one hand, and change attitudes on the other. This is discussion therapy in a community setting.

Agrin has examined "therapeutic community" treatment tactics in hospitals and clinics and found them to be more systematically practiced by professional therapists.[8] Even so, the essence of the strategy is to reduce authority roles in a clinic instead of to increase them. Much emphasis is placed on reducing barriers to communication between patients and clinic staff, patient and patient, staff and staff. This emphasis reduces the social distances between patients and authority figures and encourages a democratic atmosphere. Unlike the method used in halfway houses, usually only a minimum of rules is imposed. Thus the therapeutic community attempts to give patients more responsibility for themselves, to give low-status personnel more importance as therapeutic agents, and to reduce the role of doctors and psychiatrists in decision making about alcoholic patients. In a broader way the general strategy of the therapeutic community expands group concepts into a use of all the interpersonal relationships that surround the patient.

The basic scheme assumes three things: First, the alcoholic must learn to live with the anxieties and frustrations of ordinary, sober life without neurotically controlling others. Second, in a clinic or hospital devoted to the treatment of alcoholics, each aspect of his daily experience contributes to or detracts from his sobriety. Third, both patients and staff learn how to work out the problem of living and working together; the patients practice daily tolerance of typical, interpersonal tensions, and the staff learns how to avoid imposing regulations and controls.

In the hospital or clinic the goals of the therapeutic community are sought through numerous small groups of patients, who have volunteered to stay for at least six weeks, and a professional group therapist. Through group sessions and by individual counseling the therapist tries to understand how each alcoholic operates in his relationship with others, including all staff members and other patients. Often nurses and secretaries are included in therapy sessions. Finally, numerous other meetings are available to discuss a host of subjects related to alcohol.

Still another form of group therapy is group *psycho*therapy, in which the role of the professional therapist becomes more central. Therapy centers in the specific interaction *within* a specific small group, and is not necessarily related to the larger organization within which the group operates. Specific theories of personality development guide types of group psychotherapy. A classical psychoanalytic view, such as was described earlier, but applied to persons in small groups, may guide the group therapist. He believes that the emotional problems behind alcoholism stem from delayed emotional growth. Normal emotional development, as he sees it, is a slow growth from dependence on parental authority and care to a condition in which the individual achieves a larger degree of independence. If this process does not take place, an inadequate personality results. So the therapist uses the group as a therapeutic agent to get each member to become responsible for himself and to be free of infantile dependence.

On the other hand, the therapist may believe that the alcoholic's deficiency lies in inadequate learning about himself and his society.

In short, his "superego" is too poorly formed or too repressed. So the therapist directs exchange and discussion toward making the alcoholic more aware of society's demands and requirements and causing him to accept them as an inevitable part of living.

Finally, the group therapist can take the client-centered position in which he avoids injecting himself into the life of the members. Rather he waits for events to force the alcoholic to work out a plan of action himself, progressing at his own speed. This approach has been termed the "nondirective." It aims at using the group as a tool to define events and experiences for the alcoholic so that he changes his self-concepts and his notions about how he should act.

Group therapy of one kind or another tends to dominate the treatment of alcoholism. Fox has confirmed that many therapists believe that group therapy is particularly appropriate for alcoholics.[9] Keeping in mind the ingredients that go into producing alcoholism—a ready personality who drinks in heavy-drinking groups—this conclusion is probably true. Though some individual psychotherapy such as conditioned-reflex therapy and hypnosis have been used as a part of group-therapy practices, most therapies that at one time were individual-bound are now given a group setting.

Other specific aids to group therapy have been devised. "Psychodrama" and "sociodrama" call for the patient to act out, before others in the group, behaviors in imaginary situations that have been difficult for him. In essence these devices are role-playing techniques designed to teach the social skills needed to cope with certain situations.

Evaluation of Therapy

Though these treatment strategies seem promising, it is always the results that count. We must, therefore, ask the simple questions: Do they work? Under what conditions do certain combinations work better than others? Can response be predicted beyond chance prior to treatment? It is precisely at the point of finding a way to evaluate itself that current therapy is lacking. Therapists usually assess results *after* therapy is completed, thus losing any opportunity for before-and-after comparisons—the first necessary device for proper evaluation.

To be a genuine test, a second device, some measure of effectiveness called a criterion, should be applied before and after therapy and the results compared to determine change. How to get a criterion, i.e., measure of response, creates another problem. Will response be gauged, for example, by the degree of sobriety maintained following therapy, or will the measure be one of adjustment in key specific roles such as job, family, or both? And, if a satisfactory yardstick can be worked out and applied both before and after therapy, how can a desirable result be attributed to the therapy? Perhaps some intervening variable, such as affiliation with AA, which might not have been included in the therapy, produced the change based on the criteria.

To aid in answering these questions, a third device, a control group, is needed. The control group consists of untreated alcoholics who are as similar as possible to the treated ones before therapy. If after therapy, when the treated and untreated groups are compared on the criterion, the treated group shows improvement and the untreated does not, the change can be attributed to the therapy. If no relative improvement in the treated group is noted, the effectiveness of the therapy is called into question.

Two methods have been used to acquire a control group and an experimental (treated) group with like characteristics. First, each treated patient is matched with an untreated one on many relevant items such as age, sex, social class, progression into alcoholism, AA experience, or IQ. The paired cases are compared on the criterion both before and after therapy. Unfortunately this technique requires a large number of cases, because in the process of finding two that match on many relevant factors, many must be discarded. Another disadvantage is the lack of knowledge of many unknown variables that might be influencing change.

The second method is the random assignment of cases to a therapy group, or a control group, on the basis of stratified sampling. This method theoretically balances out the unknowns and makes for legitimate comparison of the treated with the untreated groups. It requires a knowledge of sampling and a firm policy of maintaining the random assignments once they are made. Many treatment personnel feel this is unfair to those not receiving treatment and tend to break the pattern by treating them anyway. This contaminates the design. Also, when using control groups, the evaluator must take care to consider as many factors of comparison as possible which may be pertinent to the progress of the patient. For example, one evaluation by Robson used the matching method to pair up treated and untreated alcoholics on six factors: age, sex, marital status, occupation, employment status, and time lapsed since intake.[10] Experience with AA, however, which apparently did affect treatment outcome, was not included. Under such conditions, it was difficult to determine what changes were due to the therapy and what were due to AA experience.

None of the current follow-up efforts incorporate all three essentials for good evaluation. In the first place, most of them rely chiefly on evaluation *following* therapy.[11] This leaves a blind spot in judgments about therapy effectiveness. Patients, prior to therapeutic effort, probably vary in the extent of loss of control and impairment of home and job life. If no "before" yardstick is available, the "after" rating of improvement may be misleading. Moreover, under these conditions, it is difficult to estimate the extent to which therapy may worsen rather than improve an alcoholic.

Second, most of the present evaluation studies use a criterion based only on degrees of sobriety following therapy. Usually the degrees of sobriety described are: "abstinent," "drank small amounts or intermittently with good adjustment," "frequently intoxicated," and "deceased." Only occasionally will a measure of effectiveness include other aspects of behavior such as general health, job situation, and social relationships, even though such criteria lend themselves much more readily to a before-after use than does a criterion based on sobriety alone.

Third, and equally crippling, if not more so, is the near absence of control groups in present-day evaluation of therapy. Reported evaluations repeatedly suggest the need for them, but in only one known instance has such an operation actually been systematically carried out.

Results of Evaluation

Follow-up efforts which use not all but a combination of some of the described devices, are suggestive about therapy results even if they are not conclusive. With this condition in mind, we can ask the question: What success does therapy have? Typically 30 to 40 percent of alcoholics treated with the same combination of therapies show definite improvement within one year. Using a matching type of control group in therapy evaluation, Robson has shown that this figure dropped to approximately 20 percent.[12]

Clearly these results are not spectacular. In many instances, however, the cases treated were late-stage, homeless, and jobless patients. Efforts with middle-stage, socially stable alcoholics, who are sufficiently motivated to seek treatment, should yield higher returns. This is suggested by the fact that those who do improve consistently tend to have had a steady job prior to therapy, to live in their own home or with relatives, to be married and living with a spouse, and to have experienced relatively little residential mobility.

Furthermore, certain therapies and combinations of therapies prove to be more effective than others. Follow-up studies by Hoff show Antabuse to be a particularly effective sensitizer to alcohol.[13] When use of the drug is accepted by the alcoholic and is accompanied by other therapies, especially group therapies, the percentage of favorable response has gone up significantly. In addition, Ends and Page have found that when specific kinds of group psychotherapy are compared, the "client-centered" approach appears to be more effective in changing self-concepts in a realistic direction.[14]

Finally, alcoholics with specific personality traits respond to some kinds of therapies more readily than to others. For example, Wallerstein has found that the very depressed alcoholic seems to respond to conditioned-reflex therapy but not to Antabuse.[15] Apparently certain social conditions and personality traits indicate readiness to join Alcoholics Anonymous. Thus, in an earlier study of mine, affiliates with AA showed a stronger need to establish and maintain close emotional ties with others[16] than did alcoholics not affiliated with AA. The first study also showed that affiliates had associated with fewer persons who had, they believed, stopped drinking by their own will power. Thus the affiliate was not forced to choose between imitating such a model and admitting in AA his own lack of ability to conquer his problem. A second study contrasting AA affiliates with nonaffiliates also found that those who do join have higher emotional needs to establish and maintain close relationships than do those alcoholics who, though repeatedly exposed to AA, did not join.[17] So, despite AA's effectiveness, many alcoholics are unable to affiliate—probably the majority of those exposed.

As evaluation becomes more precise, the selection of particular alcoholics for specific therapies will improve. Moreover, the combination of therapies resulting in the most improvement for all alcoholics will be more clearly identified. In sum, effective therapy for alcoholism will grow as effective evaluation grows. When the results of well-designed appraisals are used to modify treatment efforts, the percentage of successes will rise appreciably.

Strategies of Treatment

Regardless of the specific kind of therapy, there are certain basic strategies without which treatment is apt to be ineffective. First is the need for the alcoholic to remain abstinent. Despite clear evidence presented by Davies that some alcoholics have been able to return to "social drinking" and to control their tippling,[18] most make therapeutic progress by realizing that they cannot drink at all under any conditions. Only sobriety will provide them with a chance to learn to live with the anxieties and frustrations of a sober life. And they can reach a measure of sobriety only if some relaxation of anxiety is developed. This is, in effect, a vicious cycle. The cycle must be broken with a period of sobriety that sets the stage for therapy. If the belief is fostered by the alcoholic that he can return to controlled drinking, bringing about the break in the vicious cycle will be difficult. Moreover, practical experience shows with monotonous regularity that the alcoholic who tries to drink like others quickly falls back into loss of control.

The best results occur when therapies are combined; they cannot stand alone. For example, psychotherapy, whether it be group or individual, is a very slow process so that often Antabuse, conditioned-reflex therapy, or relatively safe tranquilizers may also be given to provide an adequate amount of sober time for the psychotherapy to be effective.

There is also good reason to believe that treatment fares best when it is coupled with the alcoholic's confrontation with a serious crisis growing from his excessive drinking. AA defines this point in the progression of alcoholism as "hitting bottom." The crisis may be a critical incident, such as arrest and conviction for drunken driving, or the more serious loss of family and job. At any rate, therapy seems to be helped appreciably if the alcoholic, by facing such an experience, has discovered that his life with alcohol is far more difficult and complicated than life without it.

This hitting bottom can be partly contrived; that is, therapy may bring crises to the alcoholic rather than rely on the halting, jerky caprice of circumstances to bring a sense of hitting bottom to him. One of the best examples of this is the policy of numerous American companies (described in Chapter 3) regarding alcoholic employees. First the company defines such personnel as suffering from a form of illness and provides them with opportunities for treatment as in numerous other illnesses. No stigma or prejudice attaches to their job or future, and some slips are expected, which may become a way for the sick persons to discover that they dare not drink normally. In other words, there is a "way back." If after a reasonable exposure to therapy, however, and on the basis of professional estimates the problem employee fails to improve, the company, backed by the union, will discharge the employee.

Such a policy constitutes "constructive coercion." By responding to the therapy offered, the alcoholic can find a way back, and he is not stamped with a label that is beyond removal. This is the constructive part. Yet by putting the job clearly in jeopardy and insisting on reasonable progress in therapy, a crisis is partly precipitated; this is the coercion part.

Social class and personality variables probably limit the efficacy of this treatment strategy. Since alcoholics in lower-status jobs probably have less seniority, skill, and pension rights invested in a job, their jobs may not really be threatened. Also supervisors tend to show more tolerance for the drinking behavior of low-status employees; thus the supervisors are less likely to apply a crisis strategy vigorously. Furthermore, some types of personalities respond only to the actual blow of a crisis, not to the fear of the consequences of a threatened crisis. If this is the case, a mere threat will be of little value. Despite these flaws, however, constructive coercion offers a realistic opportunity to provide a favorable prelude to actual therapy.

Evidence supporting the therapeutic value of a crisis comes from various sources. Lemere and colleagues concluded, after a study of the motives of 1,038 patients, that "few if any alcoholics decide to stop drinking until some pressure is put on them, such as threatened loss of job, family, health, or security."[19] Gerard and his associates, after a careful follow-up of a sample of 400 patients, reported that "the largest category of factors associated with becoming abstinent may be identified as 'fear motivated' "[20] Even compulsory confinement in a hospital or treatment center may be effective. Thus Selzer and Holloway report that six to seven years after involuntary treatment thirty-four of eighty-three patients were clearly improved.[21] Indirect evidence comes from the very low response to treatment among skid-row alcoholics. Their subcultural supports in the skid-row environment probably prevent them from reaching any kind of "bottom."[22]

Substantial psychiatric opinion also supports the value of crisis production in therapy. Representative is the position of Tiebout.[23] Speaking about the stance of three fellow psychiatrists he says: ". . . [they] recognize the potential motivating role of a crisis and seem to deplore a therapy which protects the individual from experiencing the leavening effect of such a crisis." Fox, a psychiatrist specializing in the treatment of alcoholics, states: "No patient will even consider giving up alcohol until the suffering it causes him is greater than the pleasure it gives him. He must lose something important to him, or at least be threatened with such a loss."[24]

These strategies rest on specific assumptions. Typically alcoholism works for the alcoholic; it provides a way of adjusting to life. It may appear to be a destructive and painful method to others, but for him it reduces a whole host of emotional stresses and needs, i.e., for recognition, response, or new experience. Until this emotional value of alcohol is reduced, therapy has little chance of succeeding.[25] Experiencing a serious crisis due to drinking acts to reduce this value. It also introduces realistic, clearly understood, negative sanctions, something lacking in American society. In a sense it serves as a socializing device, helping the alcoholic to learn and internalize inhibitions about drinking.

There is a need for honesty and consistency on the part of the "significant others" in the life of the alcoholic if the success of therapy is to be assured. No matter how thorough treatment may be, it faces crippling obstacles unless wife, boss, and intimate friends firmly and consistently support it. By keeping the problem out in the open and by recognizing and accepting the problem as it really is, the alcoholic faces influential reference points that challenge his repeated denials of a drinking problem. Often the alcoholic patient experiences rapid improvement, the sense of crisis subsides, and his insistence that nothing is wrong returns. If, however, the key people around him continue to define his problem realistically and support therapy, the sense of crisis continues. In the work world the company must consistently apply the policy, and the immediate boss and union must back it up. If this is not done, the alcoholic will manipulate the situation to avoid a clear-cut definition. There must be full agreement between management and the union to avoid the alcoholic's pitting one against the other.

One of the greatest threats to this kind of support for therapy is a group of indulgent relatives and close friends who protect the alcoholic from the realities and consequences of his abnormal drinking. The lengths to which such persons will go in order to absorb for the alcoholic the results of his overuse and to shield him from hitting bottom are almost unbelievable.

To illustrate: The parents of forty-nine-year-old "Johnny" recently phoned me to relate what they were doing about Johnny's being released from the hospital and to inquire if I had any other suggestions. They had paid Johnny's back rent at the rooming house where he previously stayed and had pestered the insurance company to cover for the holes burned in the furniture there. They had rented a room for Johnny at the YMCA, paying for two weeks in advance. They had purchased for him a $10 meal ticket, some new clothes including a suit, and put $50 for him in the bank. They had arranged with the police lieutenant to call them if he picked up Johnny so that they could bring him home and avoid a night in jail with "all kinds of people." They had also mailed Johnny a bus ticket so that he could get home from the hospital. When I suggested that they send Johnny a round-trip ticket, the parents called me inhuman, unthoughtful, and unchristian. With such a cushion of support to fall back on, why should the alcoholic respond for any length of time to any combination of therapies?

This anecdote introduces another basic need in therapy: in some way families, especially spouses, must be included in the therapy. Not only does such a move help to reduce the protective urge just described, but it provides a support for the consistent, "out-in-the-open" attitude that aids therapy. Moreover, the emotional problems of the spouse may recede with inclusion. Some clinic programs do aim at reducing both the well-meaning indulgence and the emotional problem of the spouse. One recent study clearly showed that patients whose spouses received concurrent treatment showed the most improvement.

Despite a trend toward consensus on these general ideas about therapy, there is still no agreement on who should do therapy and where it should take place. The dilemma centers around the question: To what extent is the alcoholic patient unique? General hospitals tend to believe that he is completely so and urge specialized clinics and treatment personnel. Still others insist that believing him to be unique underscores a long-standing stigma, that he can easily be hospitalized like any other ill person, and that traditional personnel such as doctors, nurses, and social workers should include the alcoholic in their regular treatment activities.

The conflict generates what Pittman and Stern term the "merry-go-round of referrals" for the alcoholic patient.[26] Social-work agencies refer alcoholics to psychiatric clinics, which are apt to refer them to a private physician or to a general hospital, who may in turn refer them to AA or to another social agency. In other words, responsibility for treatment and follow-up is not located in any specific community organization, nor is treatment lodged in specific professions or groups.

One of the basic reasons for this confusion comes from the ambivalence and moralism that generally surround the alcoholic in American society. Treatment personnel such as nurses, social workers, and doctors frequently view the alcoholic as an undesirable patient and are therefore generally reluctant to treat him. Until such basic attitudes change, consistent and soundly based treatment will be difficult. Such change does not come readily from within hospital staffs or treatment personnel. On the contrary, it comes from outside groups, usually in the form of pressures from such pivotal institutions as business and industry and from intense educational campaigns.

Evaluation of Alcohol Education

In addition to therapy, the basic principles of evaluation can and should be applied to training and education about alcohol and alcoholism. Hundreds of workshops, seminars, and training courses occur annually. "Summer Schools of Alcohol Studies," patterned after the original Yale University Summer School, now at Rutgers University, number well over a dozen. All have large attendance, numerous faculty members, and substantial budgets. Formal education about alcohol in high schools and intermediate grades occurs in practically every state in the union. Literally thousands of instances of mass-education efforts—newspaper and magazine articles, radio, and TV broadcasts, and exhibits at professional meetings—bombard the public. Yet no systematic efforts exist to determine the effectiveness of these many-sided educational efforts.

Recall that we spoke in the introduction about the "alcoholism industry"—a group of formal organizations, both voluntary and governmental, that have grown up to promote treatment and education. Much of the educational effort stems from their activities, and it is here that evaluation can profitably be developed and used. There tends to be, as in industrial training programs, a tacit belief that any action of training or education is bound to be effective. Furthermore there is often a belief that adequate evaluation lies in listening to friends and supporters give testimonials about schools and programs. As a result the organizations in this new alcoholism industry have no objective basis for improvement of their educational efforts.

Given the potency of the wet-dry struggle in recent American history, the *alcoholism industry* through training and education runs a real risk of unwittingly reviving this battle in a new form; therefore of inadvertently stimulating a "neoprohibitionism." Traditions such as the morally oriented conflict over alcohol do not change readily. For example, practically no type of training effort in America today attempts to balance the material concerning problems created by alcohol use with a realistic discussion of the positive role of alcohol in American life. Furthermore, it is quite possible that educational efforts may have an effect notably different from their avowed purposes and stated goals. Mental hygiene education, in some instances, has been known to produce unintended results. Those receiving it may come to avoid any further information, or they may project what they read and hear onto others, failing to see any self-application.

Treatment of Drug Addiction

Since the mere possession of narcotics in America is a Federal criminal offense, a very legalistic and punitive atmosphere surrounds the treatment of opiate addicts. As we have seen, the Harrison Act has been interpreted in such a manner that the medical profession avoids treating addicts, fearing prosecution. Recall that technically they are free to treat the addict. But should they be challenged by Federal agents, the question of whether or not their behavior conforms to medical standards will be resolved by a judge and jury, not by fellow professionals. Consequently the doctor does not know at the time of his efforts how he might be judged later. Under these conditions, professionally oriented treatment is largely confined to two Federal hospitals in Lexington, Kentucky, and Fort Worth, Texas, where therapy takes place under government auspices. Nonprofessional therapy, devised by addicts themselves, operates in large cities throughout the country in such organizations as Narcotics Anonymous and Synanon.

In the professionally oriented hospitals, many of the patients are voluntary; i.e., though not Federal prisoners, they have given themselves up for treatment because their tolerance is too high for the supply to be met by theft. Treatment in the hospitals usually lasts approximately four to six months. At first, either the amount of drugs used by the patient is reduced gradually in order to minimize withdrawal symptoms, or a substitute drug, Methadone, a synthetic narcotic, which causes only mild abstinence distress, is used for the same purpose. Next, in what is labeled the orientation period, a plan of therapy is worked out. During this time the hospital staff, consisting of a psychiatrist, social worker, psychologist, and vocational counselor, assesses the individual case and selects specific kinds of psychotherapy, vocational training, and work assignments. After these decisions have been made, the patient follows the prescribed regimen on a treatment ward.

Recently Dole and Nyswander describe intense exploratory work with Methadone as a substitute for opiate use by addicts.[27] Apparently the drug, although technically addictive, produces less dependency, thus permitting the addict a measure of relief from his severe dependency. Almost by accident high dosages of Methadone for addicts were substituted for heavy doses of morphine, producing an unusual decline in their yen for opiates.

Cases so treated in a research program at Rockefeller Institute in New York City showed rapid recovery with only minor withdrawal distress during absence of the drug. Tolerance did not mount rapidly, and many medical tests showed no undesirable side effects. On the other hand, these results have yet to be tried out on large samples of addicts and so are mainly suggestive.

Narcotics Anonymous, first of the nonprofessional therapy groups, is similar to Alcoholics Anonymous. Within the organization, group norms and attitudes opposed to the use of drugs replace those favoring use. Made up of ex-addicts joined together to help each other stay "clean," Narcotics Anonymous sets up certain steps similar to the twelve steps of AA. The first step reads, "We admitted we were powerless over drugs and that our lives had become unmanageable." Nyswander has described Narcotics Anonymous as an organization whose new members are recruited by a member addict's telling his story to other addicts whom he has sought out in jails and hospitals.[28] Often the newcomers are sponsored by old members, who are available to be called upon for support at any time. Regular meetings are held approximately twice a week.

Synanon, the second nonprofessional therapy group, is also an organization of former addicts. Carrying out the notion of addict-treating-addict much farther than Narcotics Anonymous, their program is aimed at the creation of a tight-knit group whose intense purpose is to alienate the addict from his subculture. Synanon seeks to give the addict definite status in, and a sense of belonging to, a group that is furiously antidrug, anticrime, and antialcohol.

To do this, Synanon operates dormitories or "Synanon houses" where addicts live under a tightly controlled program of admission, indoctrination, and status promotion. Although the basic measure for admission is a stated desire to join the group, a vigorous selection process is used to eliminate those who are merely looking for a place to "kick," to get a few free meals and lodging, or to steal. Believing that the addict is a pathological liar, leaders of Synanon use stress interviewing methods to assess the degree of willingness of the addict to submit to their group demands. Thus the applicant is taunted with harsh questions that imply he is a person bordering on insanity who desperately needs Synanon, but whom Synanon does not need. In doubtful instances his willingness to submit is tested by forcing him to cut off his hair, turn over his money, or to return a second or third time before being admitted. This description is based on a study by Volkman and Cressey.[29]

Once accepted, the newcomer, or "fish," is treated as a child in the literal sense. He is watched, cautioned, reprimanded, and exhorted by a member who is with him at all times. He is allowed to make no phone calls and write no letters. If able, he is permitted to do menial chores and slowly to take on more independent tasks, but always under the watchful eye of the "adult" member. Newcomers cannot associate with newcomers, and a severe reprimand is immediately forthcoming for junkie talk. Should a member fail to report violators, he runs a good chance of being exiled from the group. One norm is heard over and over—"Stay clean."

The best example of Synanon's utmost effort to break the addict's ties with his past and give him a conventional outlook is called, by members, the "haircut." This is a severe grilling faced by a member who deviates from the group's explicit tough expectations. Questioned by members having higher status than he, the deviant member must admit his digression openly before all members, or he must leave the group completely. A similar kind of cross-examination or seeking the simple truth takes place regularly in the evenings in small groups called synanons (from which the organization got its name), made up of six or seven rotating members.

By demonstrating over a period of time of some length—usually a year—his submission to the group and his fervent desire to be a reformer of other addicts, a member may advance from being a "child" through adolescence, young adulthood, and adulthood. In the latter category he can work on the outside, is free to marry and leave, but is still expected to return as a good example.

How effective are these various therapies? Expert observers of the hospital-based therapies believe that their major weakness lies in a lack of follow-up care after the addict's return to his home community. Underlying this concern is a belief, justified by a high relapse rate, that the treatment of addicts faces heavy odds. A follow-up study of 247 adolescent users in New York City showed that crimes.[30] Follow-up of 4,776 addicts treated at United States Public roughly 85 percent had returned to either drug use or related

Health Service hospitals at Lexington showed only 13 percent of those located (60 percent of total treated) were still abstinent.[31] A recent California study showed only 15 percent abstinent from drugs eighteen months after treatment.

In contrast, residents of Synanon appear to show higher rates of drug-free living. Of 103 members who remained at least one month in a Synanon house, 48 percent remained abstinent for at least a year; of those staying as residents at least three months, 66 percent were "clean"; and of those residing at least seven months, 86 percent were nonusers.[32] Apparently for those who stay long enough, induction into an intense antidrug organization and the subsequent taking on of the role of a therapist for other addicts tend to change addiction to drugs more than do traditional treatment methods.

SOME THOUGHTS ABOUT THE FUTURE

With an emotionally charged social problem like alcoholism the central focus is typically upon doing something *now*. Highest priorities, for instance, are currently given to efforts aimed at treatment and education about alcohol and alcoholism. But even as this takes place, it is obvious that the psychological factors of personality (we called it "readiness" earlier), operating with sociological ones (structure and values of drinking groups), are inexorably producing the next decade's alcoholics. Observations of this kind raise the question: What visible trends foreshadow the future for the *prevention* of alcoholism and drug addiction?

It seems reasonable to believe that the acceptance and use of alcoholic beverages will become more widespread. The general trend toward female drinking suggests this possibility. In addition, the clear drift away from the frontier-type swilling of early America toward the present acceptance of social drinking by the middle classes, indicates a slow but steady tendency to crystallize a more favorable social reaction to alcohol. Combined with a dramatic increase in the leisure time available to the mass of the population for drinking-related recreation and a lessening of some of the extremes of the Prohibition era, these factors augur for a definite increase in the amount of drinking.

Two results seem likely from this trend. First, the social confusion and uncertainty about the use of alcohol will slowly decline, and second, the number of ready personalities exposed to the risk of alcoholism will increase. If these factors are balanced, the potentiality for producing alcoholics in American society will probably remain roughly the same for some time to come. There is the possibility, however, that this potentiality may go up, since widespread use will make the early-stage alcoholic less conspicuous than ever and thus delay clear definition of a specific drinking problem.

A genuine hope for the future lies in a refocusing of attention away from the extreme deviation of a few skid-row-type alcoholics to the less spectacular and less dramatic, but still debilitating middle- and early-stage alcoholic. This hope can be strengthened by an awareness that the real challenging problems lie with this early- or middle-stage alcoholic, who is still a part of his community, whose family life is partly intact, and who is still in a regular job. Such a redirection of energies will prepare the way for (1) early recognition, (2) identification of alcohol problems with major institutions rather than with welfare agencies, (3) reversal of the social isolation that surrounds the developing alcoholic, and (4) the stimulation of social controls from key nonalcoholics. Moderate success in these areas would set the stage for the long-range possibilities of devising "functional equivalents" for alcohol and of accepting a type of early childhood initiation in the use of alcohol that would include in it personality-control patterns.

Early Recognition

If the early symptoms of alcoholism can be recognized as the harbingers of an obsessive and destructive illness, the chances of dealing with it effectively should be increased. Unfortunately, certain conditions restrict this assumption. Though the alcoholic is aware, even in the early problem drinking stage, that he is different and feels anxious about the problems alcohol is causing him, he continues to drink because his drinking is an immediate answer to many of these problems. In the early stages, therefore, he is not apt to do much to identify his problem. I have carried on research on two groups of alcoholics with results showing that the abnormal drinker is not likely to recognize that he must face his problem until he is well advanced into the middle symptoms.

Early identification, therefore, rests not with the alcoholic himself but with key nonalcoholics in his life such as spouse, private physicians, or immediate bosses. Wives and husbands of alcoholics, unfortunately, want to deny the problem almost as fervently as the alcoholic himself during the earlier symptoms. Doctors, as yet, are quite untrained in early detection and, even if they were sensitive, could be fooled by the alcoholic's untruths. It is the immediate boss who seems to have the greatest potential for early recognition.[1] He is less emotionally involved. Also he stands to gain from the early detection, thus avoiding absenteeism and low-quality work to be expected from a subordinate who is progressing into later stages of alcoholism. Most jobs by their very nature—schedules, routines, inspections—reveal clues of developing alcoholism to the supervisor and so facilitate early identification at the time when therapy will be more effective.

Identification of Alcohol Problems with Major Institutions

The trend toward early recognition in the work world is aided by a trend toward the association of the definition and treatment of alcoholism with pivotal institutions such as business and industry rather than with welfare agencies, mental hospitals, and jails. Because industry and business hold a central position in the power structure of American life, their influence can bring about an acceptance of alcoholism as a treatable disease. Only to the extent that business management develops realistic policies toward early- and middle-stage alcoholics and follows through with them, will traditional attitudes toward alcoholism be broken and effective action taken.

Industry, however, is supported by other institutional structures into which concern for arresting and treating alcoholism might be incorporated. If new knowledge could be practically used in general hospitals, offices of private physicians, and medical school curricula as well as in legal practice, the courts, and schools of law, the groundwork could be laid for true social change.

Efforts to reduce the stigma of alcoholism and to identify it in the early stages run a high risk of extinction unless they are channeled through such basic institutions as described above. Often in the past, large social movements aimed at the problems of alcoholism (the Washingtonians and the Blue and Red Ribbon movements of the mid-1800s) have died because they arose and tried to remain active outside influential and traditional American institutions. Such a fate could befall current voluntary and governmental agencies concerned with alcoholism. Fortunately a solid beginning has been made in many of these organizations by close cooperation with medicine and industry, without which the future might reveal a repetition of past failures.

Social Control Rather Than Social Isolation

The last two sections have suggested that social control of developing alcoholism be substituted for the social segregation and isolation process described earlier. Such a strategy involves a fundamental shift in emphasis with effective prevention coming from the reaction of key nonalcoholics toward the sufferer rather than from within the sufferer himself. If the "significant others" in the life of an alcoholic vacillate and call his malady by every conceivable name other than what it really is, they give up the chance to exercise control for conformity. If finally they do admit the reality of alcoholism but then respond with ostracism, sentimental pleading, shaming, and moral ridicule, they lose even further the opportunity to exercise a moderating influence, and they force the alcoholic into a small world of his own where he is free to develop. The hope for prevention, then, lies in the reversal of this process—that is, in trying to change the reaction of the key people in the alcoholic's life from avoidance to confrontation, from mislabeling to out-in-the-open diagnosis, and from ostracism to rehabilitative support.

Long-range Prevention

The strategies just discussed aim at relatively early social controls of problem drinking but do not carry out a program for prevention of alcoholism. To gain real prevention, efforts must be directed toward such etiological factors as reducing readiness and the social values of alcohol, and toward such unusual notions as a functional substitute for alcohol, training for use of expanding leisure time, and introducing children early in life to a controlled use of alcohol in the home.

Reducing readiness for alcoholism involves the vast field of mental health. Obviously no summary of this field is appropriate here, but it does seem practical to comment on reducing some of the things that produce readiness. Conscious efforts to adjust to authority figures such as parents, supervisors, and teachers can help to reduce the compulsive needs for independence and the anxieties that underlie them. Also, the need to show masculinity can readily be achieved in athletics and scholarship accomplishments rather than in drinking.

More important, however, are the clinical efforts, systematically and professionally undertaken by counselors in high schools and colleges and backed by community mental hygiene clinics, to help susceptible personalities. Though it is slow to come about, sufficient personnel to carry out this counseling service combined with early recognition of the potential alcoholic can probably reduce the potential of alcoholism.

Equally possible, though perhaps impractical, are efforts directed toward reducing the social prestige of the early symptoms of alcoholism, i.e., high tolerance of alcohol and blackouts. Advocates of such efforts believe that mass education about these early danger signs will cause a person experiencing them to moderate before losing control. Unfortunately the prestige of "holding your liquor" and "drinking your dinner" are so embedded in drinking folklore that early-stage alcoholics may be impervious to the influence of magazines, newspapers, and television.

The notion of functional substitutes for alcohol, such as sports, games, hobbies, travel, etc., may also be an impractical possibility.[2] Diversified recreation programs seem appropriate in isolating communities on college campuses, but in secular urban centers it seems unlikely that any substantial degree of substitution could occur short of unusual social change.

On the other hand, the rapid approach of the time when large segments of the population will have as many days of leisure as they do of work may be just the social change that forces a close examination of how young people can be prepared for the use of leisure time. With the increase of free time, the custom of drinking alcohol will either expand to fill part of this time or will accompany other forms of leisure such as bowling, boating, fishing, golf, folk singing, etc. Americans may be approaching a release from toil only to find an increased exposure to alcoholism or some other crippling addiction such as gambling. Thus it is not too early to begin to think about a type of education which, though shocking to many persons, will train young people for a healthy use of leisure time rather than for a productive vocation.

Even more controversial is the suggestion that the manner in which children experience alcohol be drastically altered. Recall that Orthodox Jewish- and Italian-Americans, despite frequent heavy use, so link the drinking of alcohol with family-connected rituals that the child comes to include it in his inhibition system as a part of the general pattern of social controls. Alcohol for the Jewish- or Italian-American is not of any value as a symbol of reaching adulthood. In contrast, the typical American child is introduced to alcohol usually late in adolescence, outside the home, often from deviant persons, and under emotionally charged conditions. Such an induction into drinking alcohol enhances the attraction of drinking-group experiences, becomes significant in proving adulthood,[3] and becomes useful as an adjustment possibility with pleasure and excitement as a by-product.

In view of the fact that most teen-agers will drink sooner or later, true prevention would seem to reside in introducing them to alcohol in a fashion that is parent- and home-related, with regular and casual exposure, and with no significance attached to its use in moderate amounts. On the other hand, such an approach assumes that the history of alcohol as a moral issue in American society could be removed, and that the deep-seated confusion about its meaning could be clarified. In practical terms it assumes that parents would take it upon themselves to introduce and expose their children to regular use of alcohol in small amounts rather than permit uncontrolled and deviant forces in the community to do so.[4] To expect that American drinking customs might become like those of Jews or Italians, we should have to assume that the entire American culture complex, within which alcohol is embedded, would basically parallel that of the other two.

It seems improbable that any of these assumptions will become fact in the immediate future. In regard to Americans drinking like Jews, actually just the reverse is happening, as we have seen in the study of Jewish alcoholics mentioned in Chapter 4. Of course it is true that changes in social attitudes toward emotionally charged behaviors have come about in the past (witness the trend in the younger generation to accept civil rights). And so today the pressures to consider the prevention of alcoholism equally as important as treatment and education may slowly force a more realistic appraisal of the ways in which children become inducted and socialized into alcohol usage.

Prevention of Opiate Addiction

If we are unrealistic in speaking of prevention of alcoholism, we are even more so in speaking of prevention of opiate addiction. Centered as it is among the most deprived segments of our population, it feeds on poverty, hopelessness, and despair. The everyday lives of addicts seem to contain more of the risks of psychopathology than do those of most people; therefore readiness for addiction is high. Above all, persons who become addicted to opiates are rejected in a compounded sense: from their communities as members of racial minorities, from their own kind because of addiction, and from society in general as criminals in a legal sense.

Under such conditions the main hope for prevention of opiate addiction in the future lies in (1) altering the criminal status of the addict so that he can be regarded as a medical problem and (2) developing a feeling within the medical profession of freedom to use professional skills in treatment efforts without fear of arrest and prosecution. If such changes can be effected, the way is clear to follow the general strategy of prevention of alcoholism and induce the medical profession to push back the point of early identification and treatment.

In England such a situation seems generally to prevail. Unlike Americans, who look upon the addict as a criminal, the English view him as a medical problem to be treated at low cost by a physician.[5] Since the addict does not have to steal or peddle drugs, his image as a criminal is further removed. There were only 335 known addicts in England in 1955, and apparently no increase in drug addiction has taken place. In the United States, a nation only about three times larger, there is an estimated minimum of approximately 60,000 addicts.

In this country a potent crime ring has enormous vested interests in increasing the number of addicts, not preventing them. Permitting doctors to treat addicts as sick persons in a medical sense would help to reduce the profits of this criminal syndicate as well as to stop the vicious cycle of drug addiction: dependency, expensive illicit supply, property crimes, and back to dependency. However, the long-standing stereotype of depraved fiend, combined with years of efforts by police and Federal agents to suppress the illicit drug traffic, make such a permission improbable.

On the other hand, both the legal and medical professions have gone on record as favoring such a general policy. In 1960 the Joint Committee on Narcotic Drugs of the American Bar Association and

American Medical Association recommended a review of laws to abolish prison terms for addicts, to allow qualified doctors to dispense narcotics, and to establish experimental out-patient clinics for their care of addicted persons.[6] A change of this kind has been supported by prominent authorities on drug addiction.

Recent pressures for reforms have been considerable. In September, 1962, President Kennedy convened a White House Conference on Narcotic and Drug Abuse. One of its main themes was to encourage state legislation (currently operating in New York and California) that would permit the arrested addict to choose treatment—usually in a government-operated facility—rather than face criminal charges for which he would probably be imprisoned. Since the criminal charge is held in abeyance, however, the punitive atmosphere and the fears of private physicians remain.

The New York State Department of Mental Hygiene has recently begun small-scale studies to determine the results of giving addicts controlled dosages. Drs. Marie Nyswander and Vincent P. Dole, of the Rockefeller Institute and Manhattan General Hospital, continue their exploratory studies of Methadone, reporting encouraging results. These efforts point toward the development of a treatment regimen available to physicians, should their fears abate.

None of these changes confront the problem of personality readiness, the massive problems of poverty and racial discrimination, or the popular stereotype of the dope fiend. They do point in the right direction, however, toward placing the treatment of drug addiction where it belongs—with the medical profession and not in a jail, court, or the United States Treasury Department.

Irony lies in the fact that the Harrison Act does not, in any way, prevent doctors from treating addicts. It is purely a revenue act. Furthermore, the Federal courts describe addiction as a disease, and a Supreme Court decision cleared the way for physicians, acting in good faith, to treat addicts legitimately. Unfortunately, administration of the Harrison Act within the United States Treasury Department has largely ignored these legal facts. Physicians continue to fear lengthy prosecution if they administer drugs in an attempt at treatment.[7]

As we have seen, these fears are of long standing among American physicians, as are the administrative practices of the Treasury Department. Consequently a slow process of authoritative influence —such as the Joint Committee referred to above—will be needed to alter administrative practice and change doctors' attitudes. Clearly there is a trend in this direction, but until the trend becomes emphatic change, we probably show unwarranted enthusiasm in speaking of prevention of drug addiction.

FOOTNOTES

Chapter One: An Overview of Main Themes

1. For an examination of social definitions of alcohol's effects see R. Freed Bales, "Cultural Differences in Rates of Alcoholism," *Quarterly Journal of Studies on Alcohol*, vol. 6, pp. 481–499, 1946.

2. Edith E. Lisanky, "The Psychological Effects of Alcohol," in Raymond G. McCarthy (ed.), *Alcohol Education for Classroom and Community*, McGraw-Hill Book Company, New York, 1964, pp. 104–121.

3. Leon A. Greenberg, "Alcohol and Emotional Behavior," in Salvatore P. Lucia (ed.), *Alcohol and Civilization*, McGraw-Hill Book Company, New York, 1963, pp. 109–120.

4. John J. Conger, "Perception, Learning and Emotion: The Role of Alcohol," *Annals of the American Academy of Political and Social Science*, vol. 315, pp. 12–21, 1958.

Chapter Two: The Social Climate

1. Joseph Gusfield, "Status Conflicts and the Changing Ideologies of the American Temperance Movement," in David J. Pittman and Charles R. Snyder (eds.), *Society, Culture and Drinking Patterns*, John Wiley & Sons, Inc., New York, 1962, p. 104.

2. Robert Straus and Selden Bacon, *Drinking in College*, Yale University Press, New Haven, Conn., 1953, p. 31.

3. Andrew Sinclair, *Prohibition: The Era of Excess*, Little, Brown and Company, Boston, 1962, p. 36.

4. Harold W. Pfautz, "The Image of Alcohol in Popular Fiction: 1900–1904 and 1946–1950," *Quarterly Journal of Studies on Alcohol*, vol. 23, pp. 131–146, 1962.

5. Kettil Bruun, "Drinking Practices and Their Social Function," in Salvatore P. Lucia (ed.), *Alcohol and Civilization*, McGraw-Hill Book Company, New York, 1963, pp. 218–227.

6. Selden Bacon, "Alcohol and Complex Society," in David J. Pittman and Charles R. Snyder (eds.), *Society, Culture and Drinking Patterns*, John Wiley & Sons, Inc., New York, 1962, pp. 78–100.

7. Harry S. Sullivan, *The Interpersonal Theory of Psychiatry*, W. W. Norton & Company, Inc., New York, 1953.

8. Leon Greenberg, "Alcohol and Emotional Behavior," in Salvatore P. Lucia (ed.), *Alcohol and Civilization*, McGraw-Hill Book Company, New York, 1963, pp. 109–120.

9. Sigmund Freud, *Civilization and Its Discontents*, The Hogarth Press, Ltd., London, 1930, p. 37.

10. Marshall Clinard, "The Public Drinking House and Society," in David J. Pittman and Charles R. Snyder (eds.), *Society, Culture and Drinking Patterns*, John Wiley & Sons, Inc., New York, 1962, pp. 270–292.

11. *Ibid.*, pp. 283–286.

12. Mark Keller, "Alcoholism: Nature and Extent of the Problem," *Annals of the American Academy of Political and Social Science*, vol. 315, pp. 1–11, 1958.

13. State of California, Department of Public Health, *Drinking Practices Study: Characteristics of Abstainers*, Berkeley, Calif., 1961. (Mimeographed.)

14. Keller, *op. cit.*, p. 4.

15. Raymond G. McCarthy, "Consumer Expenditures for Alcoholic Beverages," in Raymond G. McCarthy (ed.), *Alcohol Education for Classroom and Community*, McGraw-Hill Book Company, New York, 1964, pp. 143–146.

16. Examples of quantity-frequency studies are M. Maxwell, "Drinking Behavior in State of Washington," *Quarterly Journal of Studies on Alcohol*, vol. 13, pp. 219–239, 1952; Genevieve Knupfer et al., *Factors Related to Amount of Drinking in an Urban Community*, State of California, Department of Public Health, Report no. 6, 1963 (mimeographed); and H. A. Mulford and D. E. Miller, "Drinking in Iowa: 1, Sociocultural Distribution of Drinkers," *Quarterly Journal of Studies on Alcohol*, vol. 20, pp. 704–726, 1959.

17. Robert Straus, "To Drink or Not to Drink," in Salvatore P. Lucia (ed.), *Alcohol and Civilization*, McGraw-Hill Book Company, New York, 1963, pp. 211–216.

18. George L. Maddox, "Adolescence and Alcohol," in Raymond G. McCarthy (ed.), *Alcohol Education for Classroom and Community*, McGraw-Hill Book Company, New York, 1964, pp. 32–47.

19. Keller, *op. cit.*, p. 3.

20. Albert D. Ullman, "Sociocultural Backgrounds of Alcoholism," *Annals of the American Academy of Political and Social Science*, vol. 315, pp. 48–54, 1958.

21. John W. Riley and Charles F. Marden, "The Social Pattern of Alcoholic Drinking," *Quarterly Journal of Studies on Alcohol*, vol. 8, pp. 265–273, 1947.

22. Joseph R. Gusfield, "Status Conflicts and the Changing Ideologies of the American Temperance Movement," in David J. Pittman and Charles R. Snyder (eds.), *Society, Culture and Drinking Patterns*, John Wiley & Sons, Inc., New York, 1962, pp. 101–119.

23. Mulford and Miller, *op. cit.*, p. 725.

24. Gusfield, *op. cit.*, p. 115.

25. Robert E. Popham, "Some Social and Cultural Aspects of Alcoholism," *Canadian Psychiatric Association Journal*, vol. 4, pp. 222–228, 1959.

26. George L. Maddox and Audrey M. Jennings, "An Analysis of Fantasy," *Quarterly Journal of Studies on Alcohol*, vol. 20, pp. 334–335, 1959; see also George L. Maddox and Bernice Allen, "A Comparative Study of Social Definitions of Alcohol and Its Use among Selected Male Negro and White Undergraduates," *Quarterly Journal of Studies on Alcohol*, vol. 22, pp. 418–427, 1961.

27. Giorgio Lolli, *Alcohol in Italian Culture*, The Free Press of Glencoe, New York, 1958.

28. E. M. Jellinek, *The Disease Concept of Alcoholism*, Hillhouse Press, New Haven, Conn., 1960, p. 30.

29. Charles Snyder, *Alcohol and the Jews*, The Free Press of Glencoe, New York, 1958, pp. 3–5.

30. Milton L. Barnett, "Alcoholism in the Cantonese of New York City: An Anthropological Study," in Oskar Diethelm (ed.), *Etiology of Chronic Alcoholism*, Charles C Thomas, Publisher, Springfield, Ill., 1955, pp. 179–227.

31. Donald D. Glad, "Attitudes and Experiences of American-Jewish and American-Irish Male Youth as Related to Differences in Adult Roles of Inebriety," *Quarterly Journal of Studies on Alcohol*, vol. 8, pp. 406–472, 1947.

32. Albert Ullman, "Ethnic Differences in the First Drinking Experience," *Social Problems*, vol. 8, pp. 45–56, 1960.

33. Caradine Hooton, *What Shall We Say about Alcohol?* Abingdon Press, Nashville, Tenn., 1960, p. 127.

34. J. H. Skolnick, "The Stumbling Block: A Sociological Study of the Relationship between Selected Religious Norms and Drinking Behavior," doctoral dissertation, Yale University, New Haven, Conn., 1957.

35. For example, in a comprehensive study of college students, Mormon users of alcohol showed higher social complications due to drinking and were more likely to have been drunk from alcohol than were other religious groups. Robert Straus and Selden Bacon, *Drinking in College,* Yale University Press, New Haven, Conn., 1953, pp. 143–144 and 160–161; and Selden Bacon, "Social Settings Conducive to Alcoholism: A Sociological Approach to a Medical Problem," *Journal of the American Medical Association,* vol. 164, pp. 179–181, 1957.

36. Jellinek, *op. cit.,* pp. 38–43.

37. Dwight B. Heath, "Drinking Patterns of the Bolivian Camba," *Quarterly Journal of Studies on Alcohol,* vol. 19, pp. 491–508, 1958.

38. George Devereux, "The Function of Alcohol in Mohave Society," *Quarterly Journal of Studies on Alcohol,* vol. 9, pp. 207–251, 1948; Edwin M. Lemert, *Alcohol and the Northwest Coast Indians,* University of California Publications in Culture and Society, vol. 2, no. 6, University of California Press, Berkeley, Calif., 1954, pp. 303–406; William Mangin, "Drinking among Andean Indians," *Quarterly Journal of Studies on Alcohol,* vol. 19, pp. 55–65, 1957.

39. Edwin M. Lemert, "Forms and Pathology of Drinking in Three Polynesian Societies," *American Anthropologist,* vol. 66, pp. 361–374, 1964.

Chapter Three: What Is Alcoholism?

1. E. M. Jellinek, "Phases of Alcohol Addiction," *Quarterly Journal of Studies on Alcohol,* vol. 13, pp. 673–684, 1952.

2. H. M. Trice, "The Job Behavior of Problem Drinkers," in David J. Pittman and Charles R. Snyder (eds.), *Society, Culture and Drinking Patterns,* John Wiley & Sons, Inc., New York, 1962, pp. 493–509.

3. *Ibid.,* p. 502.

4. For a detailed research account of the symptoms of alcoholism see E. M. Jellinek, "Phases in the Drinking History of Alcoholics: Analysis of a Survey Conducted by the Official Organ of Alcoholics Anonymous," *Quarterly Journal of Studies on Alcohol,* vol. 7, pp. 1–88, 1946.

5. H. M. Trice and J. Richard Wohl, "A Rank Order Analysis of the Symptoms of Alcoholism," *Quarterly Journal of Studies on Alcohol,* vol. 19, pp. 636–648, 1958.

6. It is, however, important to keep in mind the metaphorical quality of the term "sick" when applied to behavioral symptoms such as hiding

supply and rationalizing. Here the analogy between physical illness and infractions of social rules breaks down. Perhaps it is best to think of alcoholism as made up of both behavioral deviations from expected restraints and physical symptoms that result from these. See for example, H. B. Adams, "Mental Illness or Interpersonal Behavior," *American Psychologist,* vol. 19, pp. 191–197, 1964, and Erving Goffman, *Encounters,* The Bobbs-Merrill Company, Inc., Indianapolis, Ind., p .25.

7. Harold Mulford and Donald E. Miller, "Public Definitions of the Alcoholic," *Quarterly Journal of Studies on Alcohol,* vol. 22, pp. 312–330, 1961.

8. Mark Keller, "Alcoholism: Nature and Extent of the Problem," *Annals of the American Academy of Political and Social Science,* vol. 315, pp. 1–11, 1958.

9. Wayne M. Wellman, Milton A. Maxwell et al., "Private Hospital Alcoholic Patients and the Changing Conception of the 'Typical' Alcoholic," *Quarterly Journal of Studies on Alcohol,* vol. 18, pp. 388–404, 1957.

10. Robert Straus and Selden Bacon, "Alcoholism and Social Stability," *Quarterly Journal of Studies on Alcohol,* vol. 12, pp. 231–260, 1951.

11. Trice, *op. cit.,* p. 503.

12. For example see John R. Seeley, "The W.H.O. Definition of Alcoholism," *Quarterly Journal of Studies on Alcohol,* vol. 20, pp. 352–358, 1959.

Chapter Four: Alcoholics: Vulnerable Personalities and Drinking Groups

1. The notion of prone personalities is discussed further in E. M. Jellinek, "The World and Its Bottle," *World Health,* vol. 10, pp. 4–7, 1957, and Lee N. Robins et al., "Adult Drinking Patterns of Former Problem Children," in David J. Pittman and Charles R. Snyder (eds.), *Society, Culture and Drinking Patterns,* John Wiley & Sons, Inc., New York, 1962, pp. 395–412.

2. Arnold Green, "The Middle-class Male Child and Neurosis," *American Sociological Review,* vol. 11, pp. 31–41, 1946.

3. Robin Williams, *American Society,* rev. ed., Alfred A. Knopf, Inc., New York, 1960, pp. 425–426.

4. Karen Horney, *The Neurotic Personality of Our Time,* W. W. Norton & Company, Inc., New York, 1937.

5. Charles Snyder, "Inebriety, Alcoholism, and Anomie," in Marshall B. Clinard (ed.), *Anomie and Deviant Behavior*, The Free Press of Glencoe, New York, 1964, pp. 204–205.

6. See H. A. Witkins et al., "Dependence in Alcoholics," *Quarterly Journal of Studies on Alcohol*, vol. 20, pp. 493–504, 1959; and H. Aronson and Anita Gilbert, "Preadolescent Sons of Male Alcoholics," *Archives of General Psychiatry*, vol. 8, pp. 235–241, 1963.

7. Ralph Connor, "The Self-concepts of Alcoholics," in David J. Pittman and Charles R. Snyder (eds.), *Society, Culture and Drinking Patterns*, John Wiley & Sons, Inc., New York, 1962, pp. 455–467.

8. A. D. Button, "A Study of Alcoholic Profiles on the M.M.P.I.," *Quarterly Journal of Studies on Alcohol*, vol. 17, pp. 263–281, 1956.

9. G. Lolli, *Alcohol in Italian Culture*, The Free Press of Glencoe, New York, 1958, p. 79.

10. Cf. D. C. Leighton et al., "Psychiatric Findings of the Stirling County Study," *American Journal of Psychiatry*, vol. 119, pp. 1021–1026, 1963.

11. H. M. Trice, "Alcoholism: Group Factors in Etiology and Therapy," *Human Organization*, vol. 15, pp. 33–40, 1956.

12. Everett M. Rogers, "Reference-group Influences on Student Behavior," *Quarterly Journal of Studies on Alcohol*, vol. 19, pp. 244–254, 1958.

13. Marvin Wellman, "Towards an Etiology of Alcoholism: Why Young Men Drink Too Much," *Canadian Medical Association Journal*, vol. 73, pp. 717–719, 1955.

14. Albert Ullman, "Ethnic Differences in the First Drinking Experience," *Social Problems*, vol. 8, pp. 45–56, 1960.

15. Conrad Arensberg and Solon Kimball, *Family and Community in Ireland*, Harvard University Press, Cambridge, Mass., 1940, pp. 51–60, 208–218.

16. Eugenia Hanfman, "The Life History of an Ex-alcoholic," *Quarterly Journal of Studies on Alcohol*, vol. 12, pp. 405–433, 1951.

17. Robert A. Dentler and Kai T. Erikson, "The Function of Deviance in Groups," *Social Problems*, vol. 7, pp. 98–108, 1959.

18. For a generalized description of this process see Albert K. Cohen, "The Study of Social Disorganization and Deviant Behavior," in Robert K. Merton, Leonard Broom, and Leonard S. Cottrell (eds.), *Sociology Today*, Basic Books, Inc., Publishers, New York, 1959, pp. 461–462.

19. For a discussion of "secondary deviation" see Edwin M. Lemert, "Some Aspects of a General Theory of Sociopathic Behavior," *Proceedings of Meetings of the Pacific Sociological Society*, State College of Washington, vol. 16, pp. 23–29, 1948, or Edwin M. Lemert, *Social Pathology*, McGraw-Hill Book Company, New York, 1951, pp. 75–77.

20. H. M. Trice, "The Process of Affiliation with Alcoholics Anonymous," *Quarterly Journal of Studies on Alcohol*, vol. 18, pp. 39–54, 1957.

Chapter Five: Impact on Family and Work Life

1. For a summary see Joan K. Jackson, "Alcoholism and the Family," *Annals of the American Academy of Political and Social Science*, vol. 315, pp. 90–98, 1959, and Margaret B. Bailey, "Alcoholism and Marriage: A Review of Research and Professional Literature," *Quarterly Journal of Studies on Alcohol*, vol. 22, pp. 81–97, 1961.

2. Jackson, *op. cit.*, p. 91.

3. Joan Jackson, "The Adjustment of the Family to the Crisis of Alcoholism," *Quarterly Journal of Studies on Alcohol*, vol. 15, pp. 562–586, 1954; Edwin M. Lemert, "The Occurrence and Sequence of Events in the Adjustment of Families to Alcoholism," *Quarterly Journal of Studies on Alcohol*, vol. 21, pp. 679–697, 1960; and Margaret Bailey, "Research on Alcoholism and Marriage," *Social Work Practice*, vol. 9, pp. 20–30, 1963.

4. Manfred Bleuler, "Familial and Personal Background of Chronic Alcoholics," in Oskar Diethelm (ed.), *Etiology of Chronic Alcoholism*, Charles C Thomas, Publisher, Springfield, Ill., 1955.

5. Anne Roe, "Children of Alcoholic Parents Raised in Foster Homes," in *Alcohol, Science and Society*, Yale University Press, New Haven, Conn., 1945.

6. H. Aronson and Anita Gilbert, "Preadolescent Sons of Male Alcoholics," *Archives of General Psychiatry*, vol. 8, pp. 235–241, 1963.

7. *Fortune*, January, 1960, pp. 99–102.

8. Robert Straus and Selden Bacon, "Alcoholism and Social Stability: A Study of Occupational Integration in 2,023 Male Clinic Patients," *Quarterly Journal of Studies on Alcohol*, vol. 12, pp. 231–260, 1951; and W. M. Wellman and M. A. Maxwell, "Private Hospital Alcoholic Patients and the Changing Conception of the 'Typical' Alcoholic," *Quarterly Journal of Studies on Alcohol*, vol. 18, pp. 388–404, 1957.

9. H. M. Trice, "The Job Behavior of Problem Drinkers," in David J. Pittman and Charles R. Snyder (eds.), *Society, Culture and Drinking Patterns,* John Wiley & Sons, Inc., New York, 1962, pp. 500–501.

10. H. M. Trice, "Reaction of Supervisors to Emotionally Disturbed Employees: A Study of Deviation in a Work Environment," *Journal of Occupational Medicine,* vol. 7, pp. 177–188, 1965.

11. Observer and M. A. Maxwell, "A Study of Absenteeism, Accidents, and Sickness Payments in Problem Drinkers in One Industry," *Quarterly Journal of Studies on Alcohol,* vol. 20, pp. 302–307, 1959.

12. H. M. Trice, "Alcoholic Employees: A Comparison with Psychotic, Neurotic, and 'Normal' Personnel," *Journal of Occupational Medicine,* vol. 7, pp. 94–98, 1965.

13. Observer and Maxwell, *op. cit.,* p. 305.

14. H. M. Trice, "The Job Behavior of Problem Drinkers," in David J. Pittman and Charles R. Snyder (eds.), *Society, Culture and Drinking Patterns,* John Wiley & Sons, Inc., New York, 1962, p. 504.

15. *Ibid.*

16. H. M. Trice, "Reaction of Supervisors to Emotionally Disturbed Employees," *Journal of Occupational Medicine,* vol. 7, p. 182, 1965.

17. S. Charles Franco, "Problem Drinking in Industry: Review of a Company Program," *Industrial Medicine and Surgery,* vol. 26, pp. 221–228, 1957.

18. H. M. Trice, *Alcoholism in Industry,* The Christopher D. Smithers Foundation, New York, 1963.

19. Felician Foltman, "Xerox Corporation: A Case Study in Retraining," *Management of Personnel Quarterly,* vol. 1, pp. 8–19, 1962.

20. Floyd C. Mann and Lawrence K. Williams, "Some Effects of the Changing Work Environment in the Office," *Journal of Social Issues,* vol. 18, pp. 90–101, 1962.

21. Charles A. Myers, "New Frontiers for Personnel Management," *Personnel,* vol. 41, pp. 31–38, 1964.

22. *Fortune,* January, 1960, p. 101.

Chapter Six: Opiate Addiction: A Comparison with Alcoholism

1. Harris Isbell, "Historical Development of Attitudes toward Opiate Addiction in the United States," in Seymour M. Farber and Roger M. L. Wilson (eds.), *Control of the Mind, Part II, Conflict and*

Creativity, McGraw-Hill Book Company, New York, 1963, pp. 154–169.

2. *Ibid.,* pp. 158–159.

3. *Ibid.,* p. 162.

4. Alfred R. Lindesmith, "Federal Law and Drug Addiction," *Social Problems,* vol. 7, pp. 48–57, 1959.

5. 65 Stat. 767, 21 U.S.C. 174 (1952).

6. Donald J. Cantor, "The Criminal Law and the Narcotics Problem," *Journal of Criminal Law, Criminology and Police Science,* vol. 51, pp. 516–519, 1961.

7. Marshall Clinard, *Sociology of Deviant Behavior,* rev. ed., Holt, Rinehart and Winston, Inc., New York, 1963, p. 306.

8. United Nations Expert Committee on Drugs Liable to Produce Addiction, *Reports 6–7,* World Health Organization Technical Report Series, no. 21, 1950.

9. New York City Mayor's Committee on Drug Addiction, *Report of Study of Drug Addiction among Teenagers,* New York, 1951.

10. E. M. Jellinek, *The Disease Concept of Alcoholism,* Hillhouse Press, New Haven, Conn., 1960, p. 118.

11. John A. Clausen, "Social Patterns, Personality and Adolescent Drug Use," in Alexander Leighton, John A. Clausen, and Robert N. Wilson (eds.), *Explorations in Social Psychiatry,* Basic Books, Inc., Publishers, New York, 1957, p. 234.

12. Robert A. Felix, "Medical and Legal Problems Involved in Narcotic Addiction," in *Proceedings: Medico-Legal Symposiums on Narcotic Addiction,* Law Division, American Medical Association, Chicago, 1959, pp. 32–33.

13. *Drug Addiction among Young People in Chicago,* The Illinois Institute for Juvenile Research and the Chicago Area Project, Chicago, 1953.

14. Isidor Chein and Eva Rosenfeld, "Juvenile Narcotics Use," *Law and Contemporary Problems,* vol. 22, pp. 52–69, 1957.

15. Charles Winick, "Physician Narcotic Addicts," *Social Problems,* vol. 9, pp. 174–186, 1961.

16. Isidor Chein et al., *The Road to H.: Narcotics, Delinquency and Social Policy,* Basic Books, Inc., Publishers, New York, 1964, p. 167; and Harold Finestone, "Narcotics and Criminality," *Law and Contemporary Problems,* vol. 22, pp. 71–76, 1957.

17. Joan K. Jackson, "Alcohol and Crime," in Raymond G. McCarthy (ed.), *Alcohol Education for Classroom and Community*, McGraw-Hill Book Company, New York, 1964, pp. 167–172.

18. Jellinek, *op. cit.*, p. 118.

19. Alfred R. Lindesmith, *Opiate Addiction*, Indiana University Press, Bloomington, Ind., 1947.

20. Albert K. Cohen, "Characteristics of the Lower Blue Collar Class," *Social Problems*, vol. 10, pp. 303–304, 1963.

21. Chein et al., *op. cit.*, pp. 177–192.

22. Clausen, *op. cit.*, p. 256.

23. *Ibid.*, p. 259.

24. Chein et al., *op. cit.*, pp. 216–217.

25. *Ibid.*, p. 194.

26. Harris E. Hill et al., "An M.M.P.I. Factor Analytic Study of Alcoholics, Narcotic Addicts, and Criminals," *Quarterly Journal of Studies on Alcohol*, vol. 23, pp. 411–431, 1962.

Chapter Seven: Therapies and Their Success

1. R. P. Knight, "The Dynamics and Treatment of Chronic Alcohol Addiction," *Bulletin of the Menninger Clinic*, vol. 1, pp. 233–250, 1937.

2. For an example see Harry Tiebout, "The Problem of Gaining Cooperation from the Alcoholic Patient," *Quarterly Journal of Studies on Alcohol*, vol. 8, pp. 47–54, 1947.

3. See *A Symposium on the Treatment and Rehabilitation of the Alcoholic*, New Hampshire State Program on Alcoholism, 1962, especially pp. 12, 20, 26, and 34. Also see Earl Mitchell, "Rehabilitation of the Alcoholic," *Quarterly Journal of Studies on Alcohol*, Supplement no. 1, pp. 93–100, 1961, as well as John Schaffer and Sidney Wolf, "Attitude toward Mental Hospitals as an Index of Tranquilizing Drug Activity," *Psychological Reports*, vol. 11, pp. 403–406, 1962.

4. For examples see W. L. Voegtlin, "The Treatment of Alcoholism by Establishing a Conditioned Reflex," *American Journal of the Medical Sciences*, vol. 199, pp. 802–809, 1940, and Ernest C. Miller et al., "A Method of Creating Aversion to Alcohol by Reflex Conditioning in a Group Setting," *Quarterly Journal of Studies on Alcohol*, vol. 21, pp. 424–431, 1960.

5. G. M. Winship, "Disulfiram as an Aid to Psychotherapy in the Case of an Impulsive Drinker," *Quarterly Journal of Studies on Alcohol*, vol. 18, pp. 666–672, 1957.

6. R. A. Moore, "Alcoholism in Japan," *Quarterly Journal of Studies on Alcohol*, vol. 25, pp. 142–150, 1964.

7. See H. M. Trice, "The Process of Affiliation with A.A." *Quarterly Journal of Studies on Alcohol*, vol. 18, pp. 38–54, 1957, and Irving Gellman, *The Sober Alcoholic: An Organizational Analysis of Alcoholics Anonymous*, College and University Press, New Haven, Conn., 1964.

8. Alfred Agrin, "The Georgian Clinic: A Therapeutic Community for Alcoholics," *Quarterly Journal of Studies on Alcohol*, vol. 21, pp. 113–124, 1960.

9. Ruth Fox, "Group Psychotherapy with Alcoholics," *International Journal of Group Psychotherapy*, vol. 6, pp. 19–28, 1958.

10. Reginald A. H. Robson et al., *An Evaluation of the Effect of Treatment on the Rehabilitation of Alcoholics*, Alcoholism Foundation of British Columbia, Vancouver, B.C., 1963. (Mimeographed.)

11. For example, Melvin L. Selzer and William Holloway, "A Follow-up of Alcoholics Committed to a State Hospital," *Quarterly Journal of Studies on Alcohol*, vol. 18, pp. 98–120, 1957.

12. Robson et al., *op. cit.*, p. 175.

13. Ebbe Hoff, "The Use of Disulfiram (Antabuse) in the Comprehensive Therapy of a Group of 1,020 Alcoholics," *Connecticut State Medical Journal*, vol. 19, pp. 793–798, 1955.

14. E. J. Ends and C. W. Page, "A Study of Three Types of Group Psychotherapy with Hospitalized Male Inebriates," *Quarterly Journal of Studies on Alcohol*, vol. 18, pp. 263–277, 1957.

15. Robert Wallerstein, "Comparative Study of Treatment Methods for Chronic Alcoholism," *American Journal of Psychiatry*, vol. 113, pp. 228–233, 1956.

16. Trice, *op. cit.*, p. 44.

17. H. M. Trice, "The Affiliation Motive and Readiness to Join A.A.," *Quarterly Journal of Studies on Alcohol*, vol. 20, pp. 313–320, 1959.

18. D. L. Davies, "Normal Drinking in Recovered Alcohol Addicts," *Quarterly Journal of Studies on Alcohol*, vol. 23, pp. 94–104, 1962.

19. Frederick Lemere et al., "Motivation in the Treatment of Alcoholism," *Quarterly Journal of Studies on Alcohol*, vol. 19, pp. 428–432, 1958.

20. Donald Gerard et al., "The Abstinent Alcoholic," *Archives of General Psychiatry*, vol. 6, pp. 99–111, 1962.

21. Selzer and Holloway, *op. cit.*, pp. 98–120.

22. Ernest G. Palola et al., "Alcoholism and Suicidal Behavior," in David J. Pittman and Charles R. Snyder (eds.), *Society, Culture and Drinking Behavior*, John Wiley & Sons, Inc., New York, 1962.

23. Harry M. Tiebout, "Crisis and Surrender in Treating Alcoholism," *Quarterly Journal of Studies on Alcohol*, vol. 26, pp. 496–498, 1965.

24. Ruth Fox, "Treatment of Chronic Alcoholism," *The Medical Clinics of North America*, May, 1958, pp. 805–814.

25. Harry Tiebout, "The Act of Surrender in the Therapeutic Process," *Quarterly Journal of Studies on Alcohol*, vol. 10, pp. 48–58, 1949.

26. David Pittman and Muriel Stern, *The Carousel: Hospitals, Social Agencies, and the Alcoholic*, Missouri State Division of Health, St. Louis, 1962, p. 146. (Mimeographed.)

27. Nat Hentoff, "Profiles: The Treatment of Patients, II," *New Yorker*, July 3, 1965, pp. 52–53.

28. Marie Nyswander, *The Drug Addict as Patient*, Grune & Stratton, Inc., New York, 1956, p. 144.

29. Rita Volkman and Donald R. Cressey, "Differential Association and the Rehabilitation of Drug Addicts," *American Journal of Sociology*, vol. 69, pp. 129–142, 1963.

30. John A. Clausen, "Drug Addiction," in Robert K. Merton and Robert A. Nisbet (eds.), *Contemporary Social Problems*, Harcourt, Brace & World, Inc., 1961, p. 190.

31. Michael J. Percor, "Follow-up Study of Treated Narcotic Addicts," *Public Health Reports*, Supplement 170, pp. 1–15, 1943.

32. Volkman and Cressey, *op. cit.*, p. 142.

Chapter Eight: Some Thoughts about the Future

1. H. M. Trice, "New Light on Identifying the Alcoholic Employee," *Personnel*, September–October, 1964.

2. Edwin Lemert, "Alcohol, Values, and Social Control," in David J. Pittman and Charles R. Snyder (eds.), *Society, Culture and Drinking Patterns*, John Wiley & Sons, Inc., New York, 1962, pp. 553–569.

3. George Maddox, "Teenage Drinking in the United States," in David J. Pittman and Charles R. Snyder (eds.), *Society, Culture and*

Drinking Patterns, John Wiley & Sons, Inc., New York, 1962, pp. 230–244.

4. For a thorough exploration of this position see Albert Ullman, *To Know the Difference,* St Martin's Press, Inc., New York, 1960, pp. 225–230.

5. Alfred Lindesmith, "The British System of Narcotics Control," *Law and Contemporary Problems,* vol. 22, pp. 141–143, 1957; see also Edwin Schur, "Drug Addiction under British Policy," *Social Problems,* vol. 9, pp. 156–166, 1961.

6. "Drug Addiction: Crime or Disease?" *Interim and Final Reports of the Joint Committee of the American Bar Association and the American Medical Association on Narcotic Drugs,* Indiana University Press, Bloomington, Ind., 1960.

7. Alfred Lindesmith, "Federal Law and Drug Addiction," *Social Problems,* vol. 7, pp. 48–57, 1959.

NAME INDEX

SUBJECT INDEX